Instructor's Manual

American Red Cross Infant and Preschool Aquatic Program

ISBN: 0-86536-137-1

Acknowledgments

The American Red Cross Infant and Preschool Aquatic Program is a product of the Infant and Preschool Aquatics Technical Advisory Committee. The members included:

Cathy Ferguson Brennan, M.S.
Water Safety Instructor Trainer
Greater Long Beach Chapter
Long Beach, California

Harriet Helmer
Water Safety Specialist
Mile High Chapter
Denver, Colorado

Stephen J. Langendorfer, Ph.D.
Associate Professor, School of Physical Education,
   Recreation, and Dance
Kent State University
Kent, Ohio

Ginna Lee
Water Safety Instructor Trainer
Seattle–King County Chapter
Seattle, Washington

Geraldine Giannotta Olson
Water Safety Instructor Trainer
Greater Milwaukee Chapter
Milwaukee, Wisconsin

Carolyn B. Shank, Ed.D.
Professor, Physical Education and Recreation Administration
California Polytechnic State University
San Luis Obispo, California

Suzanne Tomes
Water Safety Instructor Trainer
Cincinnati Area Chapter
Cincinnati, Ohio

National sector team members included Thomas C. Werts and Victoria A. Scott, M.P.A. The following national sector staff also provided review and assistance: Frank Carroll, John Malatak, M.S., and Suzanne Randolph, Ph.D.

The program has been reviewed by the American Academy of Pediatrics, and has been further endorsed by the Council for National Cooperation in Aquatics. In addition, Chapter 2, "The Participant: Learning and Development," has been reviewed by the National Academy of Sciences–National Research Council Commitee to Advise the American National Red Cross.

Red Cross chapters that participated in the field test included:

Central Arizona Chapter
Phoenix, Arizona

Mile High Chapter
Denver, Colorado

Delaware Chapter
Wilmington, Delaware

Indianapolis Area Chapter
Indianapolis, Indiana

Louisville Area Chapter
Louisville, Kentucky

Contents

Acknowledgments iii

Part I

Introduction 3
    Purpose of the Program 3
    Goals and Objectives 3
    Purpose and Format of the Instructor's Manual 4
    CNCA Endorsement 5

Chapter 1:   **Program Operations** 7
    Facility Management 7
    Program Administration 9

Chapter 2:   **The Participant: Learning and Development** 13
    Factors That Influence Learning in Young Children 13
    Stages of Learning 16
    Factors That Influence a Child's Development 17
    The Fearful Child 26
    Children with Disabilities 27
    Common Health and Safety Concerns 32

Part II

Chapter 3:   **Program Orientation** 37
    Scheduling 37
    Materials 37
    Presentation 38
    Suggested Outline 38

Chapter 4:   **Instructor Responsibilities** 41
    Personal Characteristics 41
    Teaching 42
    Supervision 43
    Evaluation 44

Chapter 5:   **Program Content** 47
    Holding Positions 47
    Cues 56
    Introduction to Skill Progressions 57
    Infant Skill Progression 58
    Toddler Skill Progression 71
    Preschool Skill Progression 88

Chapter 6: Teaching Aids 97
　　　　　Kickboards 99
　　　　　Personal Flotation Devices 100
　　　　　Barbells 101
　　　　　Inflatable Arm Bands 102
　　　　　Styrofoam Floats 103
　　　　　Inner Tubes 104
　　　　　Toys 105

Chapter 7: Images, Games, Songs, and Rhymes 107
　　　　　Images 107
　　　　　Games and Songs for Skill Development 108
　　　　　Water Fun 'n' Rhymes 119
　　　　　Songs and Lyrics 119

Glossary 123

Appendixes
　　　　　A— *Aquatic Activity Programs for Children*
　　　　　　　 Under the Age of Three (CNCA) 125
　　　　　B— Sample Accident Report 129
　　　　　C— 50 Ways to Say "Very Good!" 131
　　　　　D— Sample Program Orientation Flyer 133
　　　　　E— Sample Emergency Medical Information 135
　　　　　F— Sample Lesson Plans 137
　　　　　G— Sample Post-Class Letter to Parents 141
　　　　　H— Parents' Evaluation... 143
　　　　　I — Instructor Class Evaluation 145

Part I

INTRODUCTION

Purpose of the Program

The American Red Cross Infant and Preschool Aquatic Program is intended to develop in young children (6 months through 5 years) a comfort level in and around the water, as well as a readiness for learning to swim. It is important to understand that this program is *not* designed to teach children to become accomplished swimmers, or even to survive in the water on their own. The program provides information and techniques for parents to orient their children to the water and to learn how to safely supervise all water activities.

For the purposes of this program, three age group levels have been identified for skill learning progressions:

1. Infant—6–18 months
   (required parent/adult accompaniment in the water)
2. Toddler—18–36 months
   (required parent/adult accompaniment in the water)
3. Preschool—3 through 5 years
   (parent/adult accompaniment in the water is optional)

The foundation of the Infant and Preschool Aquatic Program is the basic learning progression provided for the Infant level. A toddler starts with the infant progressions until he or she is relatively proficient at those basic skills. Then, the Toddler level builds upon those skills to increase endurance and aquatic knowledge in areas appropriate for a toddler's age and readiness. Because of their increased physical and mental development, preschoolers can conceivably progress through the first two levels rather quickly and begin learning and practicing at the Preschool level, which includes combination movements and skills of increased complexity. This prepares young participants for entering the American Red Cross progressive swimming courses, Beginner through Advanced Swimmer.

Goals and Objectives

This program provides a nationally standardized aquatic program for infants and young children which will promote the following:

- **Water safety knowledge and practices—**
  - Provides a program orientation that introduces basic program guidelines related to participant safety.
  - Provides printed materials which increase parents' awareness of appropriate water safety and rescue techniques.
  - Conducts activities that practice appropriate water safety and rescue techniques.
- **Aquatic adjustment and swimming readiness skills—**
  - Introduces skills appropriate to the learning rates and readiness levels of infants and young children.

— Provides appropriate activities based on sound teaching progressions for practicing aquatic adjustment and readiness skills.
— Provides challenges and goals that promote individualized development and learning.

- **Fun and enjoyment in the water—**
  — Uses play as a basic form of learning.
  — Establishes a warm, friendly, positive atmosphere conducive to learning.
  — Incorporates the use of toys, songs, and games in the learning environment.
- **Participant socialization—**
  — Encourages interaction through games and play.
  — Encourages sharing knowledge and concerns among parents.
  — Conducts activities that require cooperation among participants.
  — Provides time in each lesson for informal, unstructured activities.
- **Parental involvement—**
  — Reinforces the parent's role in the child's learning of skills, enjoyment, and water safety.

Purpose and Format of the Instructor's Manual

This Instructor's Manual contains the necessary information to enable you, the instructor, to organize and teach an effective Infant and Preschool Aquatic Program (IPAP).

The manual consists of two parts. Part I contains information related to preparation for the program. It includes operational and administrative information for use in determining whether to begin or improve a community aquatic program to include infants, toddlers, and preschoolers. It also describes developmental characteristics and learning factors for the specific age groups involved, as well as health precautions.

Part II contains the necessary information to conduct the actual program itself. It includes: a suggested program orientation for parents and their children; instructor responsibilities and teaching styles that are appropriate for children 6 months through 5 years; the skill learning progressions for the three age group levels; a chapter devoted to teaching aids; and a chapter on games that can enhance learning activities throughout the program.

Portions of this manual were developed to be consistent with the Council for National Cooperation in Aquatics (CNCA) position statement *Aquatic Activity Programs for Children Under the Age of Three* (see Appendix A) and the American Academy of Pediatrics' *Policy Statement: Infant Swimming Programs.*

CNCA Endorsement

The Council for National Cooperation in Aquatics has for many years had specific interest and concern in aquatics for very young children. There has been a great need for nationally standardized guidelines and educational materials in this area of aquatics. It is highly appropriate that the American Red Cross has developed materials that will help parents and instructors introduce young children to the aquatic environment. These excellent materials will provide needed guidance in this popular activity, and will be of great benefit in introducing young children to the water in a safe and appropriate manner. CNCA highly approves of the American Red Cross Infant and Preschool Aquatic Program.

—Louise Priest
Executive Director, CNCA
April 1988

1 *Program Operations*

This chapter includes information about facility management and program administration that is essential for starting and running a successful aquatic program for infants and young children.

The information pertains to swimming pools only, as it is not recommended that such aquatic programs be conducted in fresh water—lakes, streams, and ponds. These bodies of water are more likely to carry harmful organisms than chlorinated pools.

Facility Management

This section includes guidelines for both initial assessment and ongoing maintenance of the physical environment where classes are to be held. Whether researching the feasibility of beginning a program for young children or evaluating how to improve an existing program, the facility must be assessed according to participants' needs.

A safe, popular aquatic program for infants and young children may require adaptations to the pool facility and/or equipment. These alterations stem from the need to meet physical and behavioral differences in the very young users of the facility and to maintain an aquatic facility that is safe for this age population.

Facility Conditions
Changing Area/Locker Room
- Skid-resistant floor surfaces are desirable in all areas including aisles and showers.
- Electrical appliances and outlets must be grounded and located in appropriate areas.
- Dry, comfortable changing tables should be available.
- Sanitary crawling area should be available.
- Adequate garbage disposal, especially for soiled diapers, is necessary.
- Adequate air circulation and warm air temperature are essential.

    Note: If designing a facility, consider placing a toilet, hair dryer, and sink at child's height.

Pool Area
- A system of securing pool entrances when class is not in session is needed to prevent entry or re-entry, especially by a young child.
- A non-skid deck surface which is regularly cleaned and maintained should be part of the area.
- A storage space for instructional aids and toys is desirable, as these should be out of sight and reach when not in use.

- Steps and other changes in the water depth should be marked with a contrasting color.
- A regular inspection schedule must be set that includes checking for and/or cleaning—
  - Ladder handrails, entry devices, and teaching platforms to prevent them from getting slippery.
  - Sharp edges or disrepair on pieces of equipment.
  - Deep areas clearly marked off with a lifeline.

  All damage must be repaired immediately.

Water Conditions

Sanitation

- Pool chemistry must meet minimum state health regulations (these vary from state to state).
- Infants and toddlers must wear plastic or training pants or suits that are snug around the legs in order to prevent feces in the pool.

Temperature

Infants and young children are more susceptible to hypothermia than older children, even at relatively warm temperatures. Measures need to be taken to keep infants and young children from getting chilled.

- Water temperature of the pool should be a minimum of 82°F (86°F preferable).
- Air temperature must be raised to at least 3°F above water temperature.
- When water and air temperature cannot be controlled adequately, limit the duration of the lesson.

Depth

Young children learn best when actively exploring the aquatic environment under their own power. When the water is too deep for children to stand safely and comfortably, seek ways to reduce the depth.

- Use a facility with a gradually sloping shallow area and/or graduated steps so that a child of average size can stand alone at waist or chest level depth.
- Construct or purchase teaching platforms on which children can stand safely.
- When the depth cannot be controlled or when participants are infants, a parent, instructor, and/or flotation device may be used to support the child.

Auditory and Visual Stimulation

Instructors need to control sights and sounds in a pool environment that can divert attention since infants and young children have a limited capability to discriminate and tolerate distractions.

- Limit loud, distorted sounds as much as possible.
- Limit the number of other children who may be moving rapidly and shouting or crying.

- Encourage persons to talk in normal voices and not shout over the noise.
- Store unused toys and equipment.
- Remove any child showing signs of overstimulation to a quieter area of the pool to calm down and adjust to the environment.

Program Administration

Program administration encompasses a variety of elements essential to starting and continuing an efficient and effective program.

Community Needs

The success of the Infant and Preschool Aquatic Program may well depend on its ability to meet community needs. A well-rounded program accommodates nap times, meal times, preschool hours, families with working parents, families in which both parents wish to participate, and families with more than one child. To help determine an effective class schedule, consider sending a questionnaire to parents through day care centers, youth swimming classes, PTAs, Sunday schools, etc.

Promotion

Promote and advertise the program to a specific population—parents of children between the ages of 6 months and 6 years—so that they become aware of the program and informed about how IPAP's specific advantages meet their family needs. Use simple, concise descriptions and include age group levels and skill progressions. Brochures, posters, local newspaper advertisements and articles, radio and television announcements all can promote participation. The Parent's Video (Stock No. 329322), which is targeted to parents for orientation, can also be used for promotional presentations.

Registration

Keep enrollment procedures simple. Schedule registration times that are convenient to both registrants and staff, and make registration available by mail. Have knowledgeable staff available on-site to answer questions regarding the program. In addition, persons answering the telephones need accurate information about the program and its schedule in order to provide adequate responses to inquiries. Have medical releases available and provide the Parent's Guide (Stock No. 329320) and handouts to be read prior to orientation, if possible. Finally, to accommodate a possible overload, consider keeping a waiting list or scheduling additional classes.

Scheduling

Class scheduling is dependent upon pool availability, community needs, staffing, and facility characteristics (water chemistry, air and water temperature, and depth). If possible, offer programs in the daytime and evenings, on weekdays and weekends.

The recommended class schedule for infant and toddler classes is 7 to 10 sessions for a maximum of 30 minutes each, at a minimum of twice a week. Classes for preschoolers may extend to 45 minutes each. Sufficient time between classes is encouraged in order to facilitate communication between instructors and parents.

The ideal teaching situation is to offer separate classes for each of the three age levels. However, a practical alternative is to combine infants and toddlers (6 months–3 years), as both levels require parent/adult accompaniment in the water.

Participant: Instructor Ratio

Adequate staff are essential for the safe operation of the program. The recommended ratios of participants to instructors include:
- Infant and/or toddler—
  6 to 8 parent/child pairs per instructor.
- Preschooler (without parent)—
  — 4 to 5 children who cannot touch the bottom per instructor, without an in-water aide.
  — 6 to 8 children who cannot touch the bottom per instructor, with an in-water aide.
  — 4 to 6 children who can touch the bottom per instructor, without an aide.
  — 8 to 10 children who can touch the bottom per instructor, with an aide.

Staffing

A highly qualified instructional staff is the result of superior knowledge and thorough training. Encourage staff to seek additional training at workshops and/or other classes.

In-service training should be held for all IPAP programs. One type of in-service training is an apprenticeship in which an inexperienced instructor co-teaches with a more experienced instructor. In addition, regular staff meetings and skill refresher sessions provide an opportunity for instructors to ask questions and discuss problems, as well as time to review lesson plans and procedures.

It is recommended that a qualified lifeguard be on the pool deck prior to the beginning of classes, staying until participants have left the pool area. At least one trained on-deck volunteer aide is desirable, who has duties different from those of the lifeguard. Instructors, lifeguards, aides, and parents must know where young children are at all times.

Emergency Action Plan

Facility managers and/or IPAP instructors who are responsible for conducting in-service training can utilize the *American Red Cross Lifeguard Training* Manual (Stock No. 321119) to strengthen the facility's Emergency Action Plan. All aquatic facilities need to have a plan of action which describes procedures to follow in both life-threatening and non life-threatening emergencies. Plans must include completion of an accident report (see Appendix B). The plan needs to be reviewed regularly by all staff. Consider simulating an emergency situation during an in-service training that includes an evaluation and performance feedback session.

Medical Histories

If a child has had a medical problem—particularly if the child is disabled—it is strongly recommended that his or her medical history be available and accessible at the pool site. Immediate access to medical information will aid emergency medical services personnel in giving appropriate care at the scene of an accident.

2 The Participant: Learning and Development

Read

The period from birth through the fifth year is one during which infants and young children undergo rapid and remarkable changes. A child's ability to think, feel, move, and play all change dramatically. Because a child's behavior differs so markedly from an adult's, it is crucial that parents and instructors understand some of these complex learning and developmental changes. This chapter summarizes some of the changes that you, as an instructor, should be aware are taking place at various stages.

Factors That Influence Learning in Young Children

The learning process is one way that parents and instructors can see how young children change. Learning encompasses the relatively permanent changes in behavior that result from practice or experience. The instructor directs this process by focusing on setting goals, encouraging practice, and providing feedback and motivation.

Factors which influence a young child's learning are largely under the control of the parent or instructor and thus are easily influenced in the home or teaching environment. However, the focus must be on the child's learning rather than on your teaching. Instruction is only one of many factors that influence learning in young children.

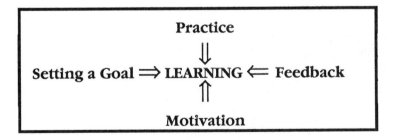

Practice
⇓
Setting a Goal ⇒ **LEARNING** ⇐ **Feedback**
⇑
Motivation

Fig. 1. Factors that Influence Learning in Young Children

Setting a Goal

To change or improve performance, the young learner must first understand the learning goal. Therefore, the first step in the learning process is to clarify this goal. Common methods for helping a child understand the learning goal include the use of the following:

- Verbal explanations (discussions, descriptions, audio tapes).
- Visual descriptions (posters, slides, video tapes, films).
- Instructor/parent demonstrations.
- Peer demonstrations.
- Physical assistance.
- Reinforcement of movements.

Each of these methods can be effective with different learners, situations, and skills.

When setting learning goals for children, the parent or instructor needs to consider factors such as these:

- Age.
- Handicapping conditions.
- Cognitive and motor skills.
- Learning stage.
- Motivation level.

For instance:

- Infants and young handicapped children may respond better to demonstrations or physical manipulations than to verbal descriptions and commands.
- Preschool age children understand fairly complex verbal instructions.
- The crying or fearful child may require a soothing, but playful, verbal description that attracts his or her interest.
- The shy child may respond better to a more enthusiastic and challenging presentation of skills.

Providing Practice

Practice is essential for improving both learning and performance of motor skills. In general, infants and young children seem to benefit most from *distributed practice,* in which frequent rest periods are distributed throughout the practice schedule. A distributed practice schedule has three important advantages:

1. It prevents fatigue.
2. It allows more time for assimilation of learning.
3. It maintains motivation and interest in the learning activity.

Applying this information to the Infant and Preschool Aquatic Program means that your classes should meet more frequently, but for shorter periods of time. For example, five classes of 20 minutes per week help young children learn more effectively than two classes of 50 minutes each.

Varied practice situations produce a stronger learning foundation than do narrow, specific, and repetitive situations. Variety and frequent rest breaks help keep children interested. For example, a child who practices several different kinds of kicks at poolside, with instructor support, and on a kickboard, is likely to learn kicking skills better than one who simply practices the flutter kick at the side of the pool.

Giving Feedback and Reinforcement

Information about how one has performed a skill is called *feedback;* *reinforcement* is the use of feedback to encourage the repetition of desired responses. Without feedback, children can make little improvement in swimming or other motor skills.

Feedback and reinforcement come from a variety of sources and can take several forms. Feedback information about swimming readiness movements can come from these sources:
- The child's own "feel" for moving in the water.
- The results of a child's movements in the water.
- The teacher and/or parent's comments about the child's skills.

All feedback is important, but its precision is particularly important. To a certain point, the more precise the information the child receives, the more beneficial that information will be in improving performance. For instance, when you simply respond "Good!" after the child has held his or her breath and submerged the face, you have provided only general feedback. It is more useful to say "Good, you held your breath with your mouth closed for two seconds. You even got your hair wet!" This precise feedback gives the child more information about what he or she or has done well. (See Appendix C for "50 Ways to Say 'Very Good!' ")

The type of information provided is important, too. This includes *knowledge of results,* such as how far or how long the skill was performed, and *knowledge of performance,* such as information about the movement pattern.

For instance, when you say "Good, you got your hair wet," or "You made it all the way across the pool kicking," you are providing knowledge of results. On the other hand, comments like "I saw your tummy when you floated on your back," or "You made nice long arm pulls," add to a child's knowledge of performance. Performance information about actual movements is especially crucial in learning an aquatic skill. Children need to know what they have done with their bodies that was successful.

Feedback is most effective when it is positive. It is much more beneficial to tell a child what he or she has done correctly than what has been done wrong. When they see a child use a kick that comes out of the water, instructors and parents may say "Don't bend your knees so much." Unfortunately, this both reinforces what the child has done incorrectly *and* fails to identify what the child should be doing. Instead, either you or the parent should say something like

"Try and straighten your knees out so you will make a smaller splash."
The instructor might provide physical assistance so that the child can
feel what using straight legs means.

Stages of Learning

As the child's experience and skill level shifts, she or he may differ in
how skills are learned. One reason for this learning difference relates
to the child's stage of learning (see Table 1). These various stages
affect goals, practice, and feedback.

The first learning stage is called the early or *cognitive* stage.
Characteristics of this stage include:
- Awkward, slow movements which seem to be consciously
  controlled by the learner.
- Poor understanding of the task.
- Little opportunity to practice.

The instructor's primary responsibilities during this early stage
include making certain that the child understands the goal of the task,
and making sure that initial attempts at a skill are successful and done
properly.

The instructor also needs to provide:
- Distributed practice.
- Corrective feedback, especially knowledge of performance.

Table 1. Characteristics of Motor Learning Stages

Name	Movement Characteristics	Intervention
Stage 1. Early or cognitive	Slow, awkward, consistent step-by-step, rigid	Get the idea of movement
Stage 2. Intermediate or associative	Variable, faster, flexible	Practice, repetition, feedback
Stage 3. Late or autonomous	Consistent, rapid, accurate, flexible	Refinement of skills, motivation

The intermediate or *associative* stage is the next stage of learning.
Children usually do not reach this stage until they have a general under-
standing of the goal of the task. Characteristics of this stage include:
- More rapid movement.
- Highly variable and inconsistent movements.
- Increased understanding of the task.
- Lack of appreciation of all the fine points that are needed to
  successfully complete the task.

At this stage, the instructor needs to provide:
- Extensive and varied practice.
- Adequate and accurate feedback to the child (both knowledge of results and of performance).

The last stage of learning is called the late or *autonomous* stage. Characteristics of this stage include:
- Accurate, rapid movements.
- Comprehension of skill technique.
- Ability to provide own general feedback.

At this stage, the instructor needs to provide:
- Minor corrections.
- Specialized feedback.
- Positive reinforcement.

In general, children do not reach the late stage of learning until they are older and more experienced than the children in the American Red Cross Infant and Preschool Aquatic Program.

Factors That Influence a Child's Development

The developmental process is another way that parents and instructors can view how young children change. Developmentally, change can be seen as behavior shifts across time. Developmental change is influenced by a child's age, heredity, experiences, and other individual differences. Developmental changes in movement, thinking, feeling, and play are especially pronounced and rapid during the early period of life.

Fig. 2. Developmental Change

Developmental Readiness

The sum total of all the child's previous experiences and developmental changes characterize the child's state of readiness. *Readiness* is the interaction of a child's age, heredity, experience, and individual differences.

The ability of the child to accept and learn new skills and tasks is limited by his or her readiness. Prerequisite skills prepare the child for the later skills. For example, children are prepared to swim underwater by their readiness to hold their breath and put their faces in the water. Such readiness is affected by the child's developmental status, age, any handicapping conditions, and experience with this skill in other situations.

Developmental Sequences

An important characteristic of development is the progressive way a child's behavior changes. A young, inexperienced child thinks and moves very differently from an older, more experienced child. For instance, many instructors may notice that a young child kicks the feet by "running" or "pedaling" in the water. After gaining more experience in the water, especially kicking, the same child moves the feet and legs to kick in other ways such as doing a flutter or breast stroke kick.

This shift in kicking behavior is an example of a developmental sequence. The earlier pedaling action is a qualitatively different type of kicking than the later flutter kick. In a developmental sense, the pedaling action is considered a rudimentary form of kicking—an early stage in the kicking sequence.

Understanding the order of developmental sequences is important to instructors and parents of young children. When adults know the order of a sequence, they can anticipate the next task or motor pattern that a child should reach. Thus, they can teach for that level.

Age and Behavior

Another important developmental characteristic is the relationship between behavior and age. With most young children, age progression is clearly related to increasing skills. An older child can do more things and do them in a more coordinated fashion than a younger one can. This is an important fact for instructors and parents of young children to know, as they can anticipate general changes and mark their child's progress by their age, among other variables.

Many instructors and parents mistakenly assume that age causes the changes they see. The child's changing body and mind, as well as increased experiences, account for these changes. Children have varying rates of learning and development. Thus, age is only a general marker of a child's developmental level. For instance, many aquatic programs for young children (including IPAP) are organized by age groups. However, a child in a younger group with more water experience may perform better than a child in an older group with less experience.

Individual Differences

Despite the similarities among young children, each one is unique. Every child has a variety of individual qualities that make him or her different: children differ in the age at which they learn new skills; they learn at different rates; and they differ in their own preferences. Instructors and parents must be sensitive to each child's unique qualities.

Another way that children differ is through their learning styles. Some children prefer to be shown how to do something through a demonstration, while others prefer to hear an explanation. Awareness of such differences is an important consideration when an instructor is planning how a skill will be presented in class. If you mostly talk about how to do something, the child who likes to see or feel how it is done may not learn as quickly.

Early Childhood Development: Tables 2–6

A young child changes in many different ways from birth through the fifth year. The following four tables list a few examples of the changes which occur during this time. For discussion purposes, the changes are arranged into the areas of *movement, thinking, feeling/perceiving,* and *play/socialization.* They are subdivided into the three levels included in this program: Infant (6–18 months), Toddler (18–36 months), and Preschool (3 through 5 years). One additional table summarizes some of the changes specific to swimming and the water.

Table 2. Changes in the Young Child's Movement from Birth to 6 Years

Characteristic	Change
Infant	
Primitive reflexes	Gradually inhibited and disappear (6 months).
Posture and equilibrium reactions	Gradually appear (4–8 months).
Voluntary motor milestones	Acquired during first 2 years.
Fine motor skills	Sequentially able to reach and grasp.
Toddler	
Voluntary gross motor skills	Begins with awkward rudimentary skills; gradually acquires smoothness; pattern improves (walk, jump, bounce jump, gallop, and run).
Fine motor skills	Grasps implements (feeding and scribbling); gradual gain in skill.
Fundamental motor skills	Rudimentary, awkward, and unskilled; little control over force or accuracy (throw, strike, and kick).
Preschooler	
Locomotor skills	Improved walking, running, jumping, and galloping; rudimentary acquisition of hopping, skipping, and sliding.
Fundamental motor skills	Gains competence in throwing, striking, and kicking; begins catching, swinging, and climbing.
Fine motor skills	Improved drawing and coloring (pictures may be recognizable); use of scissors; can begin writing letters of the alphabet.
Toy play	Can use both small and large toys in movement; rides three-wheel bike and may begin two-wheeler after fifth year.

**Table 3. Changes in the Young Child's Thinking from Birth to 6
Years**

Characteristic	Change
Infant	
Memory	Gradually shifts from immediate events to some recent occurrences.
Knowledge	Slowly links events together without action; begins to know that one event causes another event.
Object permanence	After 6 months, existence of object out of sight is understood; stranger/separation anxiety results.
Language	Sounds and babbles evolve into monosyllabic words; knows own name and names of family and common objects.
Toddler	
Memory	Greatly expanded beyond infancy. Begins to remember past; dependent upon oral memory.
Knowledge	Can abstract things; very *egocentric* (self-centered) and *animistic* (thinks all things are alive).
Language	Can say more than 20 words by second birthday, but often is hard to understand; loves repetition of stories; uses sequences of two words or more.
Preschooler	
Memory	Sense of past and future, but not like an adult; remembers through oral means; can recite jingles and rhymes.
Knowledge	Intelligence becomes more well used; fears and worries are based on primitive thinking patterns.
Language	Vocabulary includes all commonly used words, sentences, questions; can count; begins letter and word recognition; very pragmatic and literal; may not understand humor or sarcasm.

Table 4. Changes in the Young Child's Feelings and Perceptions

Characteristic	Change
Infant	
Feelings	Global, general, and without specific stimulus.
Perceptions	Linked directly to action and stimulus.
Expressions	Crying, smiling, and laughing.
Toddler	
Feelings	Rudimentary, but linked to increasing language skills; uses movement to communicate some feelings.
Perceptions	Limited discrimination of stimuli; poor selective attention; inability to integrate different senses.
Preschooler	
Feelings	Egocentric, but sometimes empathetic with others; can express some feelings vocally.
Perceptions	Increasing discrimination of stimuli levels, limited ability for attention to adult-specified tasks; begins to associate relationships across senses.

Table 5. Changes in the Young Child's Play and Socialization

Characteristic	Change
Infant	
Socialization	Limited to smiling and vocalizing through first 6 months.
Play	Manipulates objects, solitary exploration; singing can be soothing.
Toddler	
Socialization	Increases with language development; very self-centered.
Play	Solitary or parallel with other children; difficulty in sharing toys with others. Simple drills can be enjoyable; "games" in strict sense are beyond ability; enjoys songs and rhymes.
Preschooler	
Socialization	Incomplete but developing. Learning basic rules for interacting with adults and peers.
Play	Major avenue for learning and development; small groups often use dramatic and expressive play; can use simple games effectively for learning and practice.

Table 6.   Changes in the Young Child's Swimming Behavior*

Swimming Behavior	Change
Infant	
Breath control	Reflexive holding of breath changes to imitation of breathing and submerging.
Leg actions	Few spontaneous leg movements change to "pedaling" or "running" actions.
Arm actions	Arms held passively at side or overhead change to splashing or weak paddling movements.
Body position	Body position in water controlled by adult as walking on land is learned; the child holds body vertically in the water.
Toddler	
Breath control	Active submersion, bubble blowing possible; dislikes adult to control submersion.
Leg actions	Pedaling action shifts to rudimentary alternating flutter kick or frog kick action.
Arm actions	Paddling movements become alternating pulling actions with most of the force downward.
Body position	Child maintains largely vertical position in water; often dislikes back position.
Preschooler	
Breath control	Experienced preschooler can submerge for several seconds, swim underwater, and open eyes to recover objects; most children still raise head straight up out of water to get breath. Inexperienced preschooler shows fear and dislike for water in the face.
Leg actions	Alternating kick varies in effectiveness depending upon the body position; individual differences between rudimentary flutter and frog kick actions are often evident.

24

Swimming Behavior	Change
Preschooler (*continued*)	
Arm actions	Increased proficiency of arm actions is evident; experienced child is capable of using overwater recovery for rudimentary crawl, but beginner stroke is preferred.
Body position	Experienced child can use semi-horizontal position when head is submerged; when head is raised, position gets more vertical.

* Langendorfer, S., M. Roberts, and C. Ropka, "Aquatic Readiness: A Developmental Test," *National Aquatics Journal*, Vol. III No. 3, 1987, pp. 8–12.

The Fearful Child

A major challenge to aquatic instructors is dealing with young children's fearful behavior in and around the water. Infants and children often are reluctant to enter the pool environment, work with the instructor or any adult other than the parent, go into the water itself, or submerge underwater. To understand the fearful child, the instructor and parent can benefit from learning more about children's learning and development processes.

Some fears are related to the infant or young child's developmental level. At about eight months, the infant begins to express *stranger/separation anxiety*. As infants recognize the difference between a parent and others, they may react by crying and screaming or withdrawal. Some infants react by showing obvious annoyance and/or stiffening their bodies. Infants also may require extreme consistency in behavior and procedure. Failure to begin, end, or organize each lesson in similar fashion can provoke crying or reluctance to participate.

After two years of age, the child's emerging memory and *animism* may trigger fears of the unknown. The child's fantasies often can prove very distressing—to both adult and child. The imagination can conjure monsters, fearsome animals, and other distressing images. Sometimes, the child may simply be reluctant to try a new skill, but at other times, he or she may really misunderstand and fear it. In addition, the child's attraction to inanimate objects can sometimes cause him or her to reject the lesson without the presence of a favored object such as a doll, stuffed animal, or toy.

Some fears are not developmentally related, but are specifically learned from experience. For instance, a child's initial unpleasant experience with submersion may provoke fearful responses whenever an adult tries to get the child near or under the water. In addition, encouraging a child to try a new skill before she or he is prepared can evoke fear in the child when confronted with every new skill.

Social learning and developmental theories suggest ways to reduce or eliminate fearful behavior in young children. Developmentally, aquatic programs for young children must anticipate those periods when children are most likely to develop fears. The instructor should anticipate infant separation anxiety and avoid activities that require infant and parent to be separated. At later ages, other fear-related problems can likewise be reduced by careful teaching progressions, play, and attention to the child's individual needs.

Learned fears often can be avoided by anticipating possible problems. Attention to an individual child's needs, careful practice, and positive reinforcement are particularly effective. Children enjoy the water more when they can take their own time, experience success, practice repeatedly, and receive positive praise for their efforts. For example, before the young child goes under the water for the first time, it is probably important for him or her to understand what is going to happen, to be ready and agree to go under, and be told how well she or he did. Over a period of a number of lessons, the child needs to have considerable practice in holding the breath and submerging. Such a situation should reduce the child's fear.

Children with Disabilities

Infants and young children, like people of all ages, differ widely in their skills and abilities. Typical ages for many developmental levels have been discussed. However, it is widely acknowledged that these ages vary greatly from child to child. Certain conditions and variations from normal expectations are considered *disabilities* or *handicapping conditions.*

Like other children, young children with handicapping conditions vary considerably in the extent and severity of their disabilities. For example, some children with handicapping conditions are so labeled simply because they are relatively slower in developing certain skills such as sitting, walking, or grasping. Other children may have physically disabling conditions that involve abnormalities in limbs, senses, or movements. Some children who have low or slow acquisition of cognitive skills are labeled as having mental handicaps. Finally, some abnormal behaviors or responses are characterized as *behavioral disabilities.* Children may be diagnosed as having single or multiple handicapping conditions.

Children with handicapping conditions can benefit from an aquatic program and can be easily accommodated, especially with parental participation. The following table contrasts the similarities and differences between handicapped and non-handicapped children. Each child's parent is the best source of information about that child.

Table 7. Similarities/Differences Between Handicapped/Non-Handicapped Children

Similarities	Differences	Example
All children progress through essentially the same developmental changes.	Children with handicaps may be delayed in acquiring some skills and may never accomplish certain skills.	Most infants develop head control before 6 months. Handicapped infants may not have head control until several months later.
All children develop progressively, learning easier tasks first and gradually adding more difficult skills.	Children with special needs progress at slower rates and experience longer learning plateaus.	Toddlers often imitate their parents by blowing bubbles. It may take the handicapped child longer to learn this skill.
Children's performance can be measured and fit within the activities of this program.	Children with disabilities often lag significantly behind typical age norms.	Skills for younger children may be used with the disabled child.
Water activities play a part in motor, language, social, and emotional development of children.	Parents of special-needs children should consult their physician to learn any restrictions related to being in the water.	Children subject to seizures, diabetes, heart conditions, or with ear tubes may need to modify or curtail water involvement.

Common Handicapping Conditions

This section lists common handicapping conditions of infancy and early childhood, including their causes and effects. More extensive descriptions can be located in *Adapted Aquatics* (American Red Cross, 1977). Special teaching hints are included below to assist you in more effective instruction of young children with these conditions.

Mental Retardation

This condition is characterized by slow learning and a short attention span. Mentally retarded children usually demonstrate cognitive and motor skills at a less advanced level than non-handicapped children of the same age. Their learning progress often occurs at a slower rate than that of other children. Be patient, use simple phrases during instructions and demonstrations, and encourage practice and repetition.

Down's Syndrome

This chromosomal abnormality is characterized by varying degrees of mental retardation, poor muscle tone, and delayed development. Having patience, simplifying instructions, and encouraging practice are all recommended in working with children with Down's syndrome. Because these children are prone to respiratory problems, instructors

28

need to avoid chilling them during instruction, being sure to thoroughly dry their hair afterwards.

Some Down's syndrome children suffer from a condition known as atlanto-axial syndrome, which can lead to a dislocated or broken neck from flexion or extension of the neck.

Diving and swimming activities may be harmful. Before permitting these children to dive or do rolling activities, X-rays of the neck should be taken, and clearance *must* be obtained from their physicians.

Cerebral Palsy

This condition results from brain damage before, during, or following birth. This is a *physical,* not a mental, disability with limb, postural, locomotion, and speech difficulties. Cerebral palsied persons are not mentally retarded. Their problems with muscle spasticity and movement control often benefit from the buoyant and resistant characteristics of the water. They often possess very little fat tissue, however, and become chilled easily. Thus, the instructor must be observant and limit water time.

Skills on the back are usually easier for cerebral palsied children than those on the front. Flotation devices are often necessary to keep these children afloat. You also may need to provide head support to maintain breathing and head control.

Orthopedic Disabilities

These conditions involve muscle and skeletal irregularities resulting from accidental trauma (head and spinal injury), congenital malformation (spina bifida), or disease. In many cases, water can provide an important environment for exercise. If possible, involve the child's physician or physical therapist in the program.

Like cerebral palsied children, persons with orthopedic disabilities usually can perform better on the back or with flotation devices. Safety is an important concern, especially when entering or exiting the water. When the disability affects only one side of the body, stroke and skill adaptations are required. The functional limbs and body sides should be used to the best advantage.

Seizure Disorders

This term describes a wide variety of electrical brain dysfunctions ranging from unnoticeable to severe. Common types of seizures include grand mal, petit mal, psychomotor, and febrile. Seizure disorders should not prohibit a child from participating in a supervised aquatic program. In cases where seizures are poorly controlled or the child is susceptible to frequent seizures on an almost daily basis, an aquatic safety program should be undertaken with great consideration given to the risks involved since changes in temperature, fright, and other factors may trigger seizures.

When working with a child with a known seizure disorder, safety is of utmost importance. It is advisable for children to wear a personal flotation device (PFD) that allows the child to float with the face out of the water. More severe seizures involve falling and loss of consciousness; constant contact and attention are needed to avoid injury. Obviously, the water presents additional hazards since the seizure-prone individual can easily be in danger of drowning.

A child having a seizure should not be removed from the water. Do not restrain except to prevent injury. During a seizure in which the child is thrashing about, your responsibility is to keep the child away from the side of the pool and keep your hand close to the underside of the child's head to prevent inhalation of water. When the thrashing motion lapses, remove the child from the water and allow him or her to rest and become reoriented to the surroundings.

Hearing Disabilities

These include various levels of deafness or hearing impairment. How children are affected depends upon the degree of impairment, when the condition occurred, and how well they have adapted. For the most part, motor skills are not affected by hearing disabilities unless inner ear balance mechanisms are involved. In such cases, a child may have problems with posture and spatial orientation. It is important to remember that children may not be able to echo-locate where instructors are situated, so such orientation problems could be more pronounced or severe in the pool area and locker rooms.

Visual Disabilities

These range from total loss of sight to partial sightedness. Loss of vision often affects movement performance as well as a child's ability to move around a new environment. Your attention to safety around the pool is crucial. Instructors also need to use their voices effectively in describing the environment, swimming skills, and other activities. Swimming activities can be a valuable source of exercise and confidence building for the visually handicapped child.

Learning Disabilities

These include various types of impairments that often result from a neurological condition. Children with learning disabilities may exhibit a range of behaviors such as spatial relationship problems, depth perception difficulty, spatial movement problems, and clumsiness. They often have short or misdirected attention spans, are easily frustrated, overly sensitive to certain sensations, and easily fatigued. They may have difficulty taking verbal instructions, so simplifying instructions, repetition, and establishing routines are very important in teaching these children. Keeping distractions to a minimum and maintaining eye contact will help keep their attention focused.

Emotionally Disturbed (Behaviorally Disabled) Children

Children with such problems often display inappropriate behavior such as hostility, hyperactivity, or withdrawal. Such children range from mentally retarded to cognitively gifted. They are very challenging to teach since their responses are often sudden, unexpected, and inappropriate to the situation. In the water, constant attention and supervision are mandatory to ensure the safety of these children. Instructors need to establish a routine, remain calm, and be consistent in their treatment of such children. "Time outs" for certain behaviors are merited. Emotionally disturbed children often react positively to consistent positive reinforcement.

Multiple Handicaps

These are sometimes found in children with special needs and come in many different combinations. The instructor should attend to each child's individual needs. It is extremely important for you to know all of the diagnosed problems that could be related to swimming and just as important not to stereotype individuals or to underestimate what they can accomplish. As with all children—with or without handicapping conditions—safety is the first concern, followed by a water experience that is both enjoyable and educational.

Medical Clearance

It is recommended that any child with a known or suspected handicap or physical disability obtain a physician's approval to enter a water activity program. The parent must understand the risks as well as potential benefits. The risk: benefit ratio must be defined and clearly understood by both the instructor and parent. The child should not participate if the risks appear to outweigh the benefits.

Note: If a child has a medical problem, it is strongly recommended that his or her medical history be available and accessible at the pool site.

Common Health and Safety Concerns

Aquatic programs for young children have had controversy that has involved concerns about the health and safety of participants. Some concerns still remain that have not been completely resolved; these are summarized below.

Risk of Drowning

Statistically, children under the age of 6 are at greater risk of death by drowning than any other age group except young adults. The incidence of drowning by young children is primarily associated with unsupervised water situations such as bath tubs, toilets, backyard pools, and hot tubs. Nevertheless, when teaching the American Red Cross Infant and Preschool Aquatic Program, give careful attention to the safety of participants during sessions. Remind parents that even though their children may learn to propel themselves in the water, they still lack the judgment to recognize dangerous situations and/or the ability to save themselves if necessary.

Diseases and Infections

Pediatricians and other physicians generally recommend that a child who has a fever, rash, or other symptom of a bacterial or viral infection should not participate in an aquatic program. The spread of infection is generally passed from child to child by direct contact and not through the water, particularly if pool water chemistry is maintained.

Aquatic programs for infants and young children should have a clear, well-defined policy restricting participation by children and/or parents who have some contagious illness. The importance of well-maintained water chemistry also is clearly indicated in preventing the spread of infections.

Ear Infections

Ear infections are one of the most common conditions that restrict participation of young children in aquatic programs. Exposure to water commonly has been blamed for an increasing incidence of ear infections and/or worsening existing infections. In particular, children with tympanostomy tubes in the ear often have been prevented from participation in programs. Since there is disagreement among medical professionals about swimming, ear infections, and tympanostomy tubes, instructors and parents need to abide by instructions provided by their own pediatricians.

Other Water-Related Health/Physical Conditions

Two conditions related to infants and aquatic programs have received a great deal of attention in the popular and medical press. The first condition, *giardia,* is a parasitic infection which usually is transmitted through the water supply. It is most common in high altitudes and rural areas in which the water has been contaminated. There is no evidence that giardia is not controlled by standard chlorination and pool chemistry.

The second condition, *hyponatremia* (better known as "water intoxication"), has received considerable attention. Hyponatremia is an imbalance of electrolytes, especially sodium, in the bloodstream. It is an extremely rare condition.

Although hyponatremia is quite uncommon, it is recommended that young children's submersions be limited during any class session (see CNCA Statement, Appendix A).

Part II

3 *Program Orientation*

A program orientation helps prepare parents and their children for participation in the program, particularly by building their trust and confidence.

Scheduling

The orientation can either be scheduled as the first lesson of the session (without an in-water experience), or as a presentation prior to the first lesson. Attendees include parents and/or their children who are enrolled in all upcoming classes for infants, toddlers, and preschoolers. Consider scheduling the orientation to coincide with the last lesson of an IPAP class in order to demonstrate the program to new participants.

Materials

Special materials developed to orient parents to the program include the *American Red Cross Infant and Preschool Aquatic Program Parent's Guide* (Stock No. 329320) and the *American Red Cross Infant and Preschool Aquatic Program: A Good Beginning* Parent's Video (Stock No. 329322). Other materials that are recommended for use during the orientation include appropriate facility handouts. All these materials should be incorporated into an on-site presentation.

Distribute written materials to parents at registration. Request that the information be read prior to attending the orientation.

The Parent's Guide provides an introduction to the overall program, so it should be highlighted and referenced in the presentation. It includes the following information:
- Description of the program (goal and purpose).
- Answers to questions frequently asked by parents.
- Role of the Red Cross water safety instructor.
- Role of the parent.
- Skill progressions.
- Recommended readings.

The video reinforces the information in the guide. It serves as both a motivational and educational tool for the program.

Facility handouts may include the following information:
- Policies and procedures concerning the class, the facility, and its use.
- Water safety instructors and other staff and their qualifications.
- Other programs and services at the facility.

(See Appendix D for a sample facility handout.)

Presentation

°Tour

A complete tour of the facility is recommended to introduce parents and children to the changing rooms, pool (including the specific class area), equipment, toys, and the staff.

°Discussion

The topics covered in the Parent's Guide, Parent's Video, and facility handouts are all useful subjects for discussion, as are parental expectations and procedures. Explaining the purpose of the program addresses false expectations parents may have about their child's accomplishments and intent of the program. Discussing responsibilities of parents and staff alleviates concerns that might otherwise arise during the lessons. Include a brief overview of the skill progressions as listed in Appendix A of the Parent's Guide.

Certificates and Ancillary Materials

Show participants a sample of the course participation certificate (Cert. 3400) and any promotional items such as T-shirts and emblems that may be available. The certificates recognize participants' accomplishments, while promotional items give the program increased visibility in the community.

°Suggested Outline

A suggested outline for presenting the orientation is as follows:
1. Welcome and introductions.
   Introduce staff, stating qualifications to build program credibility, including:
   - All instructors assisting with the class
   - In-water and on-deck aides
   - Locker or changing room attendants
   - Lifeguards
   - Cashiers
   - Facility and/or program manager

2. Review program goal and purpose.
   A. Purpose is to develop in young children:
      - Comfort level in and around the water
      - Readiness for learning to swim
   B. Goal is to provide a nationally standardized aquatic program for infants, toddlers, and preschoolers that will promote the following:
      - Water safety knowledge and practices
      - Aquatic adjustment and swimming readiness skills
      - Fun and enjoyment in the water
      - Participant socialization
      - Parental involvement

3. Show *American Red Cross Infant and Preschool Aquatic Program: A Good Beginning* Parent's Video (Stock No. 329322), 9 minutes.

4. Highlight the *American Red Cross Infant and Preschool Aquatic Program Parent's Guide*, particularly—
   A. Chapter 3:
      "Your Instructor" (instructor responsibilities)
   B. Chapter 4:
      "How You Can Help" (parental responsibilities)

5. Review facility policies and procedures.
   A. Schedule:
      - Session starting and ending dates
      - Number and length of lessons
      - Days of the week and time of day classes are held
      - Alternate class times in case of conflicts with naps or other activities
      - Length of class period
      - Arrival and departure times for each class (these should provide an unhurried atmosphere)
      - Make-up days (if available)
      - Absence policy
      - Refund policy
      - Promotion of other facilities and American Red Cross Health and Safety classes available
   B. Class rules:
      (These rules and regulations are especially pertinent to a class of young children and their parents.)
      - Parent and child may enter the water only on the instructor's cue
      - Child enters the water only on the parent's cue
      - Both parent and child stay with the class and follow the instructor's guidance
      - The instructor is in charge at all times
   C. Appropriate swimming apparel and gear:
      - Swimsuits for parents should withstand tugging and stretching by little hands and feet
      - Swimsuits for children should be snug around the legs, or they should wear training pants underneath suits
      - Facility policy on bathing caps as applies to length of hair, not sex
      - Goggles are not recommended as they generally do not fit young children properly
      - Jewelry and watches are not to be worn
      - Disposable or thick cloth diapers are not to be worn
      - Enough towels should be brought for both parent and child
   D. Health and medical information:
      - Obtain medical release (as directed by facility management) and/or Emergency Medical Information (Appendix E)

- Require physician's written approval for known medical problems
- Discuss risks and benefits of aquatic activities with individual parents as needed
- Stipulate daily class health requirement—no one with a cough, cold, fever, infection, open sore, rash, or who looks or acts sick can participate

E. Facility rules:
- Parental supervision of children
- Safe behavior in the changing rooms
- Use of equipment
- Food, drink, and gum
- Showering
- Arrival times
- Pool rules (walking on deck, no diving areas, etc.)
- Emergency action plan

6. Question-and-answer session

7. Facility tour

With an effective orientation, parents and children will be more knowledgeable about and interested in the program. In addition, it will be easier to enforce rules and regulations. Most importantly, the experience will be positive and enjoyable for parents, children, and staff.

4 *Instructor Responsibilities*

As a Red Cross water safety instructor, your role as a teacher of infants, toddlers, and preschoolers will be different from your role as an instructor of older children and adults. Both the young age of the child and the presence of parents in class will ensure new, challenging situations. For these reasons, it is important that instructors adopt a teaching style that is appropriate for very young children.

It is essential that you feel comfortable working with both children and adults. A sincere, friendly manner is important. You will need to create a positive, trusting relationship with all participants—parents and children alike. Such relationships are likely to develop as parents and instructors cooperatively encourage children to face new, exciting challenges.

Trust is established through repeated positive experiences in which young children rely on others to help them. When parents participate with their children in the water, your role is to teach them how to work with their children, increase their safety awareness, and emphasize the benefits of safe water play. It is important to instill self-confidence in both parents and children.

The following sections discuss some of the desirable personal qualities of program instructors, as well as the major instructional responsibilities—teaching, supervision, and evaluation.

Personal Characteristics

Certain personal qualities can enhance the effectiveness of every infant and preschool aquatics instructor. Some of these are common to instructors of all Red Cross courses (see *Instructor Candidate's Manual for the Introduction to Health Services Education* [IHSE] [Stock No. 321252]). Following are characteristics which are essential for IPAP instructors in particular.

Leadership
Instructors must provide direction to parents and encourage appropriate guidance. In addition, instructors of infants, toddlers, and preschoolers must serve as positive role models to both parents and students.

Communication Skills
Effective communication with young children occurs when a child interprets the instructor's message exactly as intended. Communication can be challenging, since you need to communicate on two levels—adult and child—often simultaneously.

Patience
Due to the young ages of the children and their unique developmental levels, patience is both a necessity and a virtue. Often, instructors must deal with divergent parenting styles and beliefs, which can be quite demanding.

Flexibility
Awareness of individual differences among both adults and children requires flexibility and encourages creativity in responses and behaviors.

Health and Fitness
Since young children are susceptible to common viral infections and other contagious diseases, it is crucial for an instructor to maintain an optimal level of health and fitness.

Teaching

The IPAP instructor has numerous responsibilities which encompass the three main instructional areas of teaching, supervision, and evaluation. By developing an appropriate lesson plan, the instructor generates an outline that covers most, if not all, teaching responsibilities.

Preparing Lesson Plans
Comprehensive lesson plans serve as a blueprint for successful teaching. Regardless of an individual's teaching style, an effective instructor uses a lesson plan in class. Lesson plans organize basic class procedures and techniques, provide a guide for teaching skills and progressions, and provide vital information to a substitute or class aide. (Refer to Appendix F for sample lesson plans for the first two sessions at each level.) In general, lesson plans should be organized to include the following activities.

Warm-Up
The warm-up period helps both parent and child prepare for the rest of the lesson and includes water adjustment procedures. Welcoming and effectively introducing the child to the class setting sets a positive tone for the whole session. Be aware that the parent often adopts the attitudes and techniques demonstrated by the instructor, whom they view as the expert.

Review
This period is for practice and review of previously presented skills and information. It offers an opportunity to reinforce the skills previously learned and sets the stage for learning new skills and progressions. There should be time for the parent and child to practice familiar skills. Children learn at their own individual pace. The review period gives learners additional practice time to master a skill.

New Materials and Safety Skills

This part of the lesson includes introduction of new skills using explanations, demonstrations, or other activities. Both parents and children must understand the intent or goal of the new skill or material being introduced. New materials should be introduced after class members have learned and accomplished prerequisite materials.

Skill acquisition can be viewed like building blocks, with more fundamental skills being introduced and learned before more advanced and complex skills are taught. When the young child has mastered the foundational building blocks, he or she has acquired readiness for the next skill. The safety skills should always be introduced as part of the lesson.

Practice

During practice, new materials and skills are exercised, repeated, and reinforced. This period is an important phase in the learning process. It is necessary to present and then practice skills for young children in a fun and playful manner. Class activities should consist of drills, games, songs, and rhymes that children enjoy (see Chapter 7).

Give individualized attention and instruction to participants throughout this activity. Instructors and parents can lose their patience with young children. Remember that a child needs frequent encouragement to try or repeat skills.

Taper Off

The end of the class session is as important as the warm-up period. End each class in a consistent manner, with a favorite game or song. During this part of the lesson, children can explore new and interesting aspects of the water on their own with less adult direction. Adults also can share information with each other at this time.

Supervision

Careful, safe supervision of participants and the pool area while children are in or around the water must be maintained. An instructor provides structure and organization for the water learning environment. Structure can be imposed through specific safety rules for the class.

The varied developmental and skill levels of IPAP classes presents difficult organizational and supervisory challenges. One strategy is to bring the class together, briefly present or demonstrate a new skill, and then break up for individual practice. This can be repeated several times throughout any lesson. Another strategy is the "assembly line" method.

In infant and toddler classes, the instructor must make certain that the parent stays with the young child at all times. In preschool classes, the instructor and/or aides must know the whereabouts of all class members at all times. Young children can move very quickly and it takes only a few seconds of parental or instructor distraction for a child to get into a dangerous situation.

Setting Reasonable Goals with Parents

Instructors need to help parents set realistic goals for their child's progress in the water. Often, parents are either too lenient or too demanding of young children. Part of the instructor's supervisory role is to observe parents and children together and assess the appropriateness of the interaction. Sometimes parents need to be reminded of the variations in learning rates among children.

Providing Reinforcement

Another characteristic of the learning process is the need for feedback and reinforcement. The instructor's challenge is to provide both parents and children with specific information about their performance. Reinforcement must be immediate, positive, and constructive to be most effective. The instructor provides a good role model by complimenting parents on specific, positive actions. As a result, a parent may be more likely to pass praise along to the child.

Maintaining Records

One aspect of both class operation and overall program supervision is appropriate class recordkeeping. The instructor is responsible for taking regular attendance, noting absences, and recording student progress. Records are necessary from both a legal liability standpoint and a teaching perspective.

Evaluation

Participant Evaluation

Pre-Assessment

Evaluation is an ongoing process used to assist the instructor in determining the child's performance and progress. The evaluation process begins with a pre-assessment. The main purpose is to provide the instructor with an idea of the skills and performance levels of each child. This knowledge permits the instructor to focus on the abilities of each child.

In-Class Assessments

Throughout the class sessions, conduct informal assessments of each child's performance. Using this process, the instructor observes that some children need more repetition of skills, while other children are ready to go on to more advanced techniques. This knowledge encourages the instructor to individualize the teaching process to accommodate each child.

Post-Assessment

Include a post-assessment at the end of the session. The post-assessment evaluation indicates what skills have been learned and when particular children are ready to move on to more advanced skills. This information may be reported by a letter to parents (see Appendix G). Remember, students are awarded participation certificates; they are not evaluated on a pass-or-fail basis.

Program Evaluation

Appendix H contains an example of a course evaluation for parents. This evaluation, or a similar one used by your local Red Cross unit, should be given to participants before they leave the class to find out how they felt about the course. Appendix I contains two copies of the instructor class evaluation, which asks your opinion about this Instructor's Manual and course materials. You should fill it out the **first** and **fourth** times that you teach this course and send it directly to American Red Cross national headquarters. (The address is on the evaluation.) The information will help evaluate how well the course materials work for both new and experienced instructors.

For many instructors, teaching in the American Red Cross Infant and Preschool Aquatic Program will be a new and challenging experience. However, as this chapter has demonstrated, many of the skills learned as part of the Water Safety Instructor course apply equally well to this program. Where there are special situations, instructors need to utilize suitable methods, supervision techniques, and evaluation procedures in order to to make the program safe and enjoyable for all participants.

5 *Program Content*

This chapter describes the skills and learning progressions appropriate for the three age groups of children enrolled in the American Red Cross Infant and Preschool Aquatic Program. These skills are the building blocks for the swimming skills taught in American Red Cross Beginner through Advanced Swimmer courses.

The activities found in the infant and toddler progressions focus on the parent and child as one learning unit, as generally, such very young children have not yet learned to interact in groups. The preschool progression is designed for the child to experience a structured program without direct parent contact, which is compatible with overall preschool or prekindergarten educational philosophy.

When children are introduced to an aquatic environment, optimal learning will take place when they feel secure enough to play, practice, and progress at their own pace. The skills listed in this chapter are presented in a general sequential order. This order is not absolute and can be altered to accommodate individual differences.

It is your responsibility as the water safety instructor to systematically introduce new concepts and skills in a manner appropriate to the child's ability and readiness. You must also provide parental guidance so that adults can help their children accomplish these skills.

It is crucial to remember that, as the instructor, you are responsible for both parents and children. Do not relax safety procedures once parents are in the water with their children, as parents may not be comfortable in an aquatic environment.

Holding Positions

The following holding positions provide support and reassurance to the child while he or she explores the water and learns and practices new skills. The names of the positions reflect either what they look like or where the child's body is supported by the adult.

"Name of Position" (left) column also indicates the level at which the holding position is first introduced:
- [I] = Infant
- [T] = Toddler
- [P] = Preschool

The "Technique" (center) column describes the placement of the child in relation to the adult's body, and where the adult's hands must be placed to give the greatest physical support. This column also indicates the water level recommended to obtain the greatest skill effectiveness. The "Use" (right) column gives the specific skill(s) for which each holding position is used.

Name of Position and Level Where Introduced	Technique	Use
Dance [I]	Child straddles adult's hip. Adult's arm supports child's back by holding child at upper thigh. Adult's free hand holds child's hand. Water level: depends on use.	Water adjustment Bubble blowing Entry Exit

Hug [I]	Child's arms rest loosely around adult's shoulders. Child's legs extended, with adult supporting thighs and knees. Water level: Child's upper chest, shoulder level.	Water adjustment Front kick

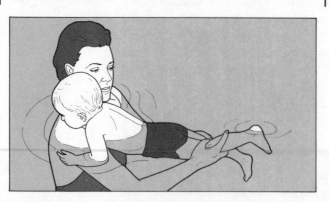

Name of Position and Level Where Introduced	Technique	Use
Face-to-Face	*Note:* The face-to-face holding positions introduce the child to prone skills.	
Face-to-Face: Chin Support [I]	Adult's fingers and palms hold infant under upper chest and shoulders; infant's chin rests on heels of adult's palms to prevent face from accidentally submerging. Water level: Child's chin, adult's shoulders.	Front kick Bubble blowing

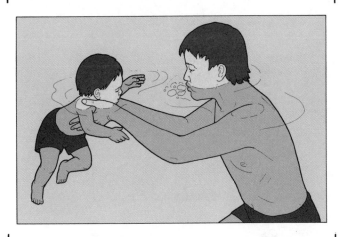

Face-to-Face: Shoulder Support [T]	Adult supports child at hip and abdomen in horizontal position; child's shoulders rest on adult's forearms.	Water adjustment Front kick Prone glide Prone float Bubble blowing

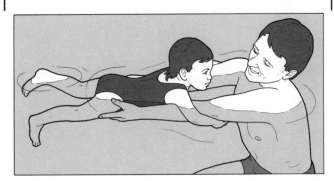

Name of Position and Level Where Introduced	**Technique**	**Use**
Face-to-Face: Armpit Support [I]	Adult's hands hold child under armpits, arms extended. Depending on size of child and use, hands will either be grasping the top of child's shoulders and back with thumbs down or grasping underneath the arms and upper chest with thumbs up. Water level: Child's chin.	Water adjustment Prone kick Prone glide Bubble blowing Underwater exploration Rolling over Drafting

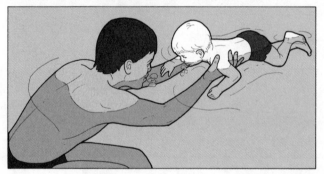

Name of Position and Level Where Introduced	Technique	Use
Arm Stroke [I]	Child sits on adult's knee, facing away. One arm keeps child upright by holding child's chest and other hand holds child's forearm to manipulate child's arms. Adult can balance child on knee and guide both arms. For leverage, adult can brace back against side of pool, sit on steps, or kneel on one knee in shallow water. Water level: Child's upper chest, armpit.	Arm movement

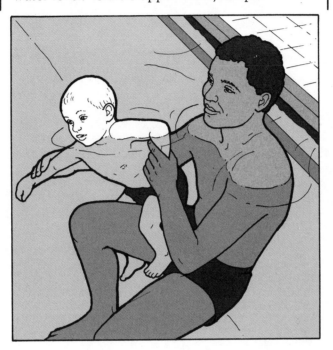

Name of Position and Level Where Introduced	Technique	Use
Side-to-Side [I]	Child is placed to one side of adult, hands holding child at armpits to keep head up. Depending on size of child, the arm/elbow of the arm going across child's back can rest against child's buttocks and legs to keep them underwater. For more support of the head-up position, this same arm can encircle child and be placed on the child's chest. As child progresses, adult holds child with both hands on waist. Water level: Child's chin or neck.	Water adjustment Bubble blowing Front kick Beginner stroke Passing Combined skills

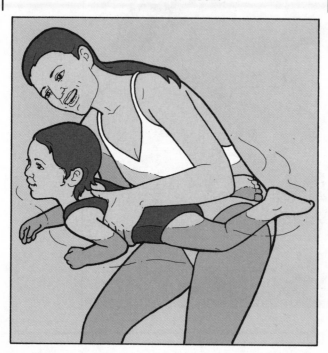

Name of Position and Level Where Introduced	Technique	Use
Cheek-to-Cheek	*Note:* The cheek-to-cheek holding positions introduce children to skills performed on the back.	
Cheek-to-Cheek: Back to Chest Support [I]	Back of child's head rests on adult's shoulder, child's cheek (side of head) touching adult's cheek. Adult leans backward against wall, supporting child on adult's chest to bring child to a horizontal position. Adult secures child with one or both hands on top of child's chest. Water level: Adult's shoulders.	Back float and back glide readiness

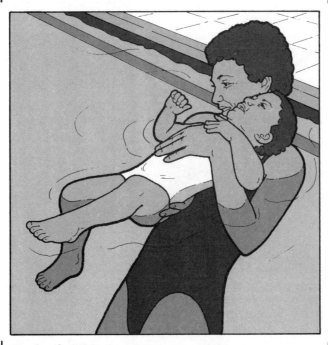

Cheek-to-Cheek: Sandwich [T]	Back of child's head rests on adult's shoulder, child's cheek (side of head) touching adult's cheek. Adult secures child in horizontal position by "sandwiching" child between adult's hands. One hand is placed on child's lower back and the other hand on child's chest. Water level: Adult's neck, child's ears.	Back float and back glide readiness Rolling over

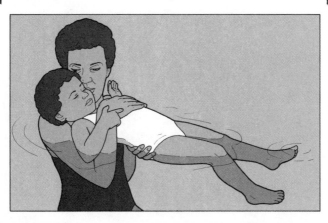

Name of Position and Level Where Introduced	Technique	Use
Cheek-to-Cheek: Back Support [I]	Back of child's head rests on adult's shoulder, child's cheek (side of head) touching adult's cheek. Adult holds child in horizontal position with both hands on the back to bring the body to a horizontal position. Water level: Adult's neck, child's ears.	Back float and back glide readiness Back kick

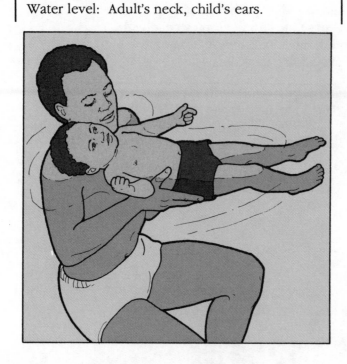

Note: Location of the adult's hand placement on the child's back is determined by child's readiness and the specific skill. Hands placed on the child's lower back lend the most support; hand placement on the upper back allows less support, thus, more freedom of movement.

Name of Position and Level Where Introduced	**Technique**	**Use**
Neck and Back Support [I]	Child moves into horizontal position on the back while adult holds child with one hand supporting the back of child's neck and other hand assists and lifts the child to a horizontal position. Water level: Child's ears.	Freedom of movement Back float and back glide readiness Combined skills

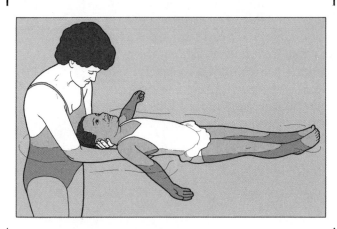

Chin and Back Support [T]	Adult supports child in horizontal position on the back with one hand while other hand is around chin on the jaw bone. *Caution:* do not push on fleshy part of throat. Water level: Child's ears.	Back float Back glide Back kick Combined skills

Note: To get the child accustomed to the feeling of buoyancy—water lifting and supporting the body—move forward or backward while holding the child as he or she practices a propulsive skill such as the prone glide or back glide.

Cues

Infants and young children need cues to understand what is expected of them. Cue words are used before initiating skills and activities. They are presented as each skill is learned and then repeated whenever that skill is practiced.

Cues are especially important for alerting the child to hold his or her breath in preparation for going underwater. For example, during the initial learning phase of the prone glide, the head stays up and out of the water, even though the end result includes the face in the water. Throughout the entire skill progression—which may take several sessions at the same or different level—it is important to use cues so the child will eventually understand and start holding hold his or her breath when the familiar cue is heard, regardless of whether his or her face actually goes in the water.

Examples of cues include:
- Ready? Set. Go!
- One, two, three . . . look back and push off!
- Ready? One, two, three . . . Jump!
- Ready—and—reach!

When using cue words or phrases, remember the following points:
- A cue must precede each skill.
- The same cue should be used before the same skill is practiced.
- Cues need to be simple and direct.
- Cues are most effective if spoken rhythmically and slowly.

If the child has been taught to wait for cues before certain activities such as entering the water, the number of unexpected and potentially dangerous situations will be minimized. Remind parents to reinforce using cue words at home when their children are around the water.

Introduction to Skill Progressions

Many skill names used throughout the following skill progressions will provide you with a familiar point of reference and not necessarily a specific end result. For instance, the back float is not required until the American Red Cross Intermediate Swimmer course. For the purposes of the IPAP program, however, it is used in a general sense to get the child adjusted to other skills that are performed in a similar position and to prepare the child for the actual back float.

In the following progressions for the three age groups, the "Skill" (left) column names the activity and lists the appropriate holding position; the "Teaching Notes" (center) column gives specific points to use when teaching this skill and giving guidance to the parent; and the "Results" (right) column describes the objective of that specific activity.

Infant Skill Progression
(6 months to 18 months)

Objectives

As a result of participating in this program, infants and parents will:

- Be exposed to water adjustment activities.
- Experience supported movement and other basic skills in the water.
- Be introduced to appropriate water safety skills.

Caution: Do not allow infants to exceed three (3) submersions per class during the adjustment and initial learning phases of the skills introduced at this level.

Skill (Positions)	Teaching Notes	Results

A. Water Adjustment	1. Getting wet—
	  • Parent and infant sit on deck and get water on each other's bodies using tub toys, washcloths, etc.
	  • Infant kicks water at edge of pool with parent's support.
	
	Safety hint: Support infant on deck to keep him or her from falling backward.
	
	2. Getting in from steps, ramp, ladder or side of pool—
	  • From steps or ramp: walk into water using dance position.
	  • From ladder: instructor supports infant on pool edge while parent uses ladder and then lifts infant into water.
	  • From side of pool: instructor or parent supports infant while parent rolls over onto stomach and slides into water. Parent then lifts infant into water.
		Readiness for entry

(Dance; Face-to-Face: Shoulder Support)	3. Exploring pool—
	  • Parent and infant explore teaching area, allowing water to flow around and past infant.
	  • Water level is parent's shoulder height.
		Awareness of surroundings

B. Water Entry

Note: Practice the following entry skills without submersion during initial learning phase. Do not allow infant underwater until adjusted to "Scooping" (see "F. Underwater Exploration").

1. Seated—
   • Parent is standing in water in front of infant seated on side of pool.
   • Give underwater cue; lift infant off side and into water.
   • Parent turns infant back to wall and places infant's hands to hold onto side of pool.

Safety

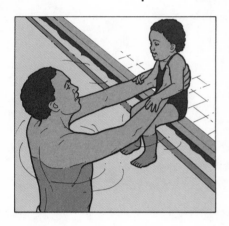
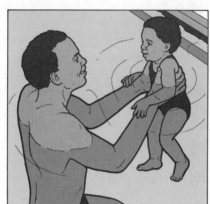
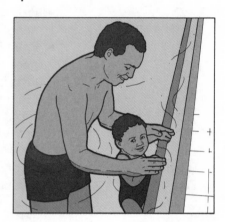

2. Jumping in—
   (When infants are able to stand independently.) Stand infant at edge of pool, supported under the infant's armpits by parent standing in water. Parent, using underwater cue, lifts infant into water. Parent turns infant back to wall and places infant's hands to hold onto side of pool.

Safety hints: Infant enters water only on parent's cue. Keep a careful grip on infant to prevent slipping or falling backward.

C. Front Kick (Hug; Face-to-Face: Shoulder Support)

- Parent moves backward.
- Use verbal cues of "kick, kick."
- Allow for natural leg movement.
- Parent can move infant's legs in up-and-down action.

Leg movement

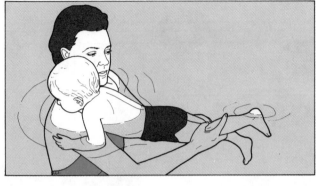

D. Bubble Blowing (Dance; All Face-to-Face Positions)

- Parent demonstrates to infant while using humming sounds and blowing bubbles gently on cheek or hand.
- Infant eventually imitates parent blowing bubbles. Practice while stationary and moving backward.

Safety hints: Keep infant from drinking water and avoid accidental submersion.

Breath control

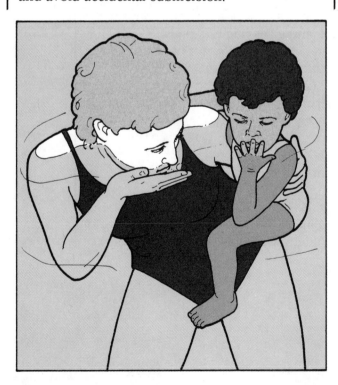

Skill (Positions)	Teaching Notes	Results

E. Prone Glide
    (Hug; All
    Face-to-Face
    Positions)

1. Readiness—
   • Parent lowers to shoulder depth and walks backward, talking or humming to infant.
   • Repeat, adding bubble blowing demonstration.

Experience
  water support

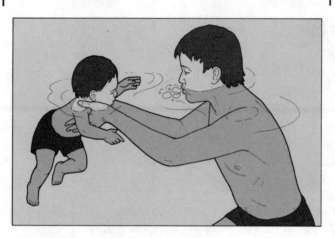

(Side-to-Side)

2. Passing—
   • (Head up) Instructor passes infant to parent only.
   • Use cue for underwater.
   • Instructor moves forward to gain momentum and gently glides and releases infant to parent.
   • Parent gains control of infant, scoops to chest, and gives hug and praise.
   • (Head down) When infant has become adjusted to "Scooping" (see "F. Underwater Exploration"), allow head to go underwater; repeat above process.
   • Pass only 2–3 feet.
   • Parent glides infant to wall, securing hands onto side of pool.
   • Parent passes infant to another adult.

Safety hints: Avoid quick or jerky movements; avoid lifting infant totally out of water; and avoid "shoving" infant toward wall or other adult.

Independent
  movement

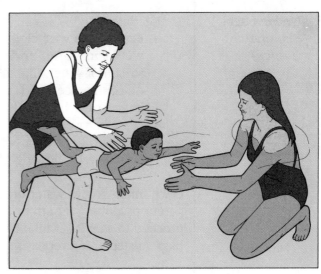

(Face-to-Face: Armpit Support)

3. Drafting—
    • Introduce this skill after infant is comfortable "passing" with face in the water.
    • As parent and infant gain momentum, moving backward, parent gives underwater cue and briefly releases support so that infant moves forward, free-floating between parent's outstretched arms.
    • Parent returns support by grasping shoulders or armpits and giving hug and praise.
    • Infant may be unsupported with face in water for a maximum of 3 seconds.

Safety hints: Avoid collisions with other parents by spreading out. Watch for infants expelling air bubbles, as response will be to inhale immediately. Do not use this skill with an infant who cries, chokes, or shows discomfort.

Do **not** exceed a total of three (3) submersions per class during initial learning phase.

Controlled free glide/float

F. Underwater
    Exploration
    (Dance)

1. Readiness—
    • Parents use washcloth or sponge to wet infant's arms and shoulders with stream of water, like taking a bath.
    • As confidence builds, let water fall a few inches onto back of head.
    • Let water wash down face.
    • Work up to point at which child can accept water flowing gently across face.

    Once infant enjoys water on face and can imitate parent by putting mouth or face in water, proceed to step 2. If infant objects or cries, go back to step 1 and repeat sequence.

Underwater adjustment

(Face-to-Face:
Armpit
Support)

2. Scooping—
    • (Head up) Using a cue, parent takes one or two steps backward, while tipping infant's head down, buttocks up, and goes through a scooping motion.
    • (Head down) When infant is ready, give underwater cue and tip infant's head so forehead or bridge of nose enters water first to avoid forcing water up nose.
    • In one continuous motion, lower infant just under water's surface and scoop up to chest. Give hug and praise.
    • Repeat skill only once during any given lesson until infant is comfortable, i.e., no crying, coughing, or choking.

Breath control

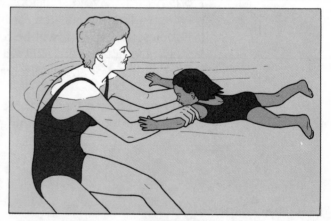

Safety hint: Infants' first reaction to going underwater may be to hold their breath. After a period of time, infants may expel air and then immediately inhale, thus taking in water. Watch for air bubbles. Be alert for forceful parents. Remind parents to keep both feet on pool bottom; caution against forcing child or keeping infant under longer than a brief "dip" (maximum 3 seconds).

Skill (Positions)	Teaching Notes	Results
G. Back Float (Cheek-to-Cheek: Sandwich; Back-to-Chest)	1. Adjustment to water in back position— • Parent lowers shoulders into water. • Infant rests head on parent's shoulder. • Parent talks, hums. • Infant's legs remain still. • Parent remains motionless or slowly moves backward.	Safety and relaxation

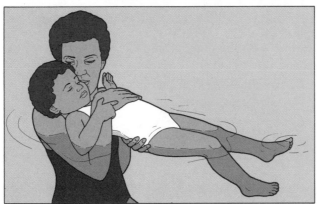

(Cheek-to-
Cheek:
Back Support)

2. Back float readiness—
    • Parent talks to infant and looks into eyes
      while moving backward.

Safety hint: Parent must watch infant's
face constantly. Avoid moving into other parents
and infants.

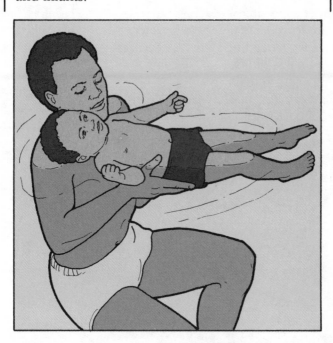

Skill (Positions)	Teaching Notes	Results

H. Arm Movement, Prone Position (Arm Stroke; Side-to-Side)

- Parent guides infant's arms, using cue such as "reach," "paddle," "dig," etc.

Safety hints: Instructor needs to watch that child's face doesn't go in the water. In side-to-side position, check that buttocks remain under surface of water to keep head up.

Beginner stroke readiness

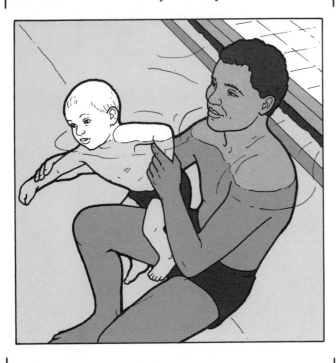

I. Combined Skills, Prone Position (Side-to-Side)

Parent moves infant through the water cueing for a combination of the following: bubbles, kicking, arm movement.

Coordinated movement

J. Rolling Over (Cheek-to-Cheek: Sandwich)

1. Rolling back to front—
   - Parent holds infant in cheek-to-cheek: sandwich position.
   - Parent cues infant and rotates hands while rolling infant onto stomach with head up.

Safety

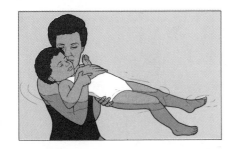  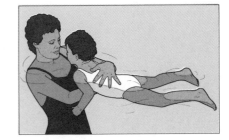

- Parent's hands move to hold infant in face-to-face position.
- Parent moves backward to gently glide infant.
- Parent encourages infant to grab wall.

2. Rolling front to back—
   - Infant is in face-to-face position.
   - Parent reaches directly across and grasps infant's upper arm, thumb down, fingers on top.
   - Fingers of the other hand hold infant under the armpit and chest while the thumb (up) holds the upper arm.
   - While moving backward, parent cues infant to roll over.
   - Parent rolls infant onto back.
   - Parent moves hands to neck and back position and cues infant to look into parent's eyes.

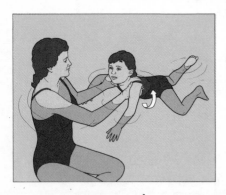
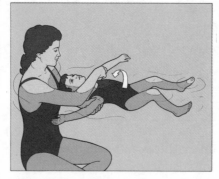
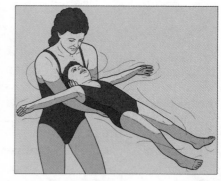

K. Parent Safety

- Parent practices basic safety skills: reaching, extension, throwing, and wading assists to other parents and/or instructor.

Safety awareness

- Parents and older infants should experience wearing PFDs, if appropriate sizes are available.

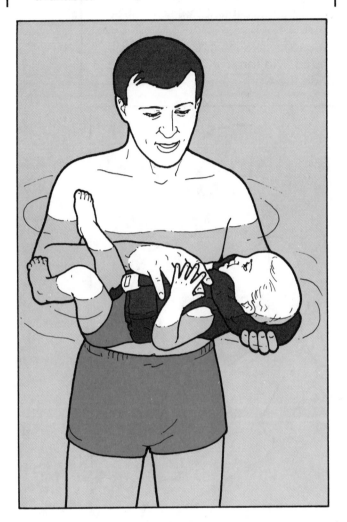

Safety hint: Use the buddy system to care for infant while parent practices assists.

L. Water Exit   1. From ladder—   Safety
                            - Parent lifts infant and sits him or her on deck next to ladder while instructor holds infant.
                            - Instructor holds child while parent uses ladder to exit pool.

2. From side—
   - Parent assists older infant in climbing out of pool, using knee or hand as step.
   - Parent helps older infant pull self out of pool.
   - Parent encourages infant to climb out unassisted. No forceful boosting; let the infant do the work.

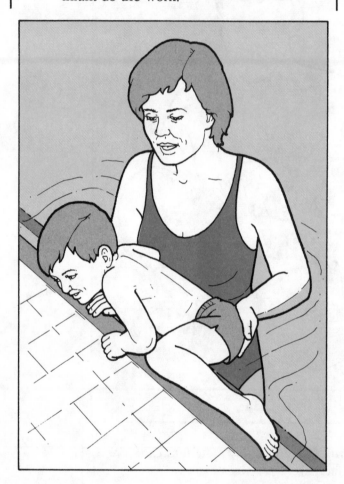

Toddler Skill Progression
(18 months to 36 months)

The toddler learning progression of this program expands upon the skills introduced at the Infant level. The toddler first learns the skills at the Infant level, then begins to develop aquatic independence at the Toddler level and is encouraged to initiate actions by verbal cues from parents and instructors.

The instructor will be challenged by the increasing individual differences among toddlers. This means that you will simultaneously continue and expand upon Infant and Toddler level skills while providing additional challenges (see Preschool level) who has already acquired many of these skills.

Objectives

As a result of participating in this course, the toddler and parent will:
- Be exposed to water adjustment activities.
- Practice elementary forms of propulsive aquatic movements.
- Observe and practice safe and effective use of flotation devices.
- Experience appropriate water safety skills.

Caution: Do not allow the toddler to exceed three (3) submersions per class during the initial learning phase.

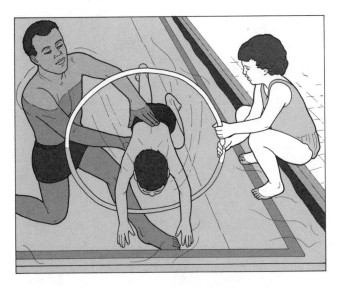

Skill (Positions)	Teaching Notes	Results
A. Water Adjustment	1. Getting wet— • Parent and toddler sit on deck and get water on each other's bodies using tub toys, washcloths, etc. • Toddler kicks water at edge of pool with parent's support.	Readiness for entry

2. Getting in from steps, ramp, ladder
   or side of pool—
   • From steps or ramp: walk into water using
     dance position.
   • From ladder: instructor supports toddler
     on pool edge while parent enters water
     and then lifts toddler into water. Stronger
     toddlers can use ladder with supervision.

- From side of pool: parent rolls over onto stomach and slides into water. Parent cues toddler to roll over onto stomach and then to enter water, holding onto side of pool.

(Dance;
Face-to-Face:
Shoulder
Support)

3. Exploring pool—
- Parent and toddler explore teaching area, allowing water to flow around and past toddler.
- Water level is parent's shoulder height.

Awareness of
surroundings

Skill (Positions)	Teaching Notes	Results

B. Water Entry

Note: Practice the following entry skills without submersion during initial learning phase. Do not allow toddler underwater until adjusted to "Scooping" (see "F. Underwater Exploration").

1. Seated—
    - Toddler sits on edge of pool.
    - Parent stands in water facing child and grasps toddler's wrists or forearms.
    - Parent gives cue and toddler jumps to parent.
    - Parent and toddler return to side.
    - Parent places toddler's hands on side of pool.
    - Repeat, using one hand to assist.
2. Jumping in—
    - Toddler stands at edge of pool.
    - Parent stands to the side of toddler, holding top of one of child's wrists or forearms.
    - Parent gives cue and toddler steps or jumps into water.
    - Parent rotates toddler, using one or both hands to return to wall.

Safety hint: Toddler jumps straight out from wall without turning; parent can assist by holding hand(s), but should not catch the toddler.

Safety

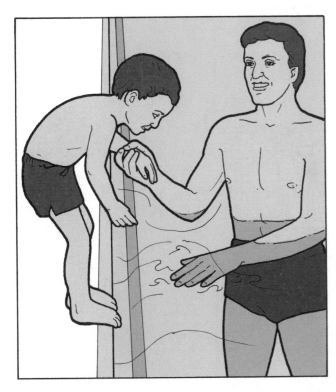
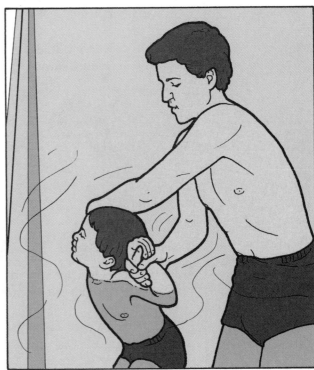

Skill (Positions)	Teaching Notes	Results

C. Front Kick
(Hug;
Face-to-Face:
Shoulder
Support)

- Parent moves backward.
- Use verbal cues of "kick, kick."
- Allow for natural leg movement.
- Parent can move toddler's legs in up-and-down action.
- With parent's assistance, toddler is encouraged to kick on own.
- Parent holds toddler's hands on kickboard or barbells.
- Parent gradually lessens support and contact.
- Cue bubble blowing as additional skill.

Leg movement

Independence

Proper use of
   flotation device
Coordination

D. Bubble
Blowing
(Dance; All
Face-to-Face
Positions)

- Parent demonstrates to toddler while using humming sounds and blowing bubbles gently on cheek or hand.
- Toddler eventually imitates parent blowing bubbles. Practice while stationary and moving backward.

Safety hints: Keep toddler from drinking water and avoid accidental submersion.

Breath control

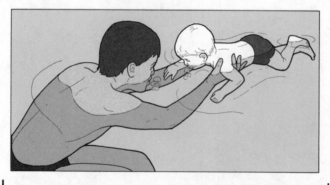

(Face-to-Face:
Shoulder or
Armpit
Support;
Hug)

- Parent holds toddler's hands onto edge of pool as toddler submerges (bobs) and blows bubbles.
- Toddler bobs rhythmically, once every 2 or 3 seconds. Discourage child from wiping water off eyes.

Visual awareness,
   safety

Skill (Positions)	Teaching Notes	Results

E. Prone Glide
   (Hug; All
   Face-to-Face
   Positions)

1. Readiness—
   • Parent lowers to shoulder depth and walks backward, talking or humming to toddler.
   • Repeat, adding bubble blowing demonstration.

Experience water support

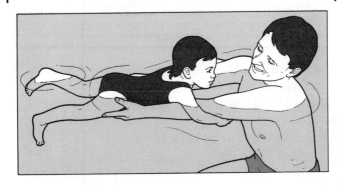

(Side-to-Side)

2. Passing—
   • (Head up) Instructor passes toddler to parent only.
   • Instructor gives cue, moves forward to gain momentum, and glides and releases toddler to parent.
   • Parent gains control of toddler, scoops to chest, and gives hug and praise.
   • (Head down) When toddler has become adjusted to "Scooping" (see "F. Underwater Exploration"), allow head to go underwater; repeat above process.
   • Pass only 2–3 feet.
   • Glide toddler to wall through hula hoop.

Independent movement

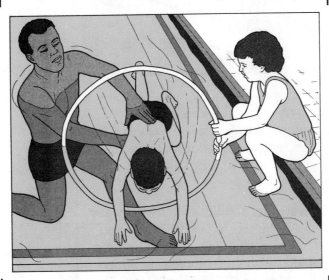

   • Parent passes toddler to another adult.

Safety hints: Avoid quick or jerky movements; avoid lifting toddler totally out of water; and avoid "shoving" toddler toward wall or other adult.

(Face-to-Face: Armpit Support)

3. Drafting—
   - Introduce this skill after toddler is comfortable "passing" with face in the water.
   - As parent and toddler gain momentum, moving backward, parent gives underwater cue and briefly releases support so that toddler moves forward, free-floating between parent's outstretched arms.
   - Parent returns support by grasping shoulders or armpits and giving hug and praise.
   - When ready, toddler may be unsupported with face in water for a maximum of 3 seconds.

Controlled free glide/float

4. Drafting with breathing—
   - Parent drafts toddler and counts to 3 seconds; parent's hand supports under toddler's shoulder or chest, cues to breathe, and lifts chin with other hand for breath.

Forward movement
Buoyancy

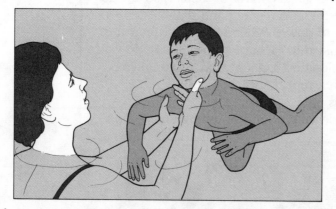

5. Glide—
   - Parent gives cue and glides toddler to wall. Parent secures child's hands to wall.
   - Toddler stands facing pool wall, pushes off from bottom, and glides to wall with parent's assistance.

Safety hints: Watch for toddler swallowing water or getting water up nose. Avoid collisions with other parents by spreading out. Do not use this skill with a toddler who cries, chokes, or shows discomfort. Do **not** exceed a total of three (3) submersions per class during initial learning phase.

Skill (Positions)	Teaching Notes	Results
F. Underwater Exploration (Dance)	1. Readiness— • Parents use washcloth or sponge to wet toddler's arms and shoulders with stream of water, like taking a bath. • As confidence builds, let water fall a few inches onto back of head. • Let water wash down face. • Work up to point at which child can accept water flowing gently across face. 2. Bubble blowing— Practice bubble blowing.	Underwater adjustment and perception
(Face-to-Face: Armpit Support)	3. Scooping— • (Head up) Using a cue, parent takes one or two steps backward, while tipping toddler's head down, buttocks up, and goes through a scooping motion. • (Head down) When toddler is ready, give underwater cue and tip toddler's head so forehead or bridge of nose enters water first to avoid forcing water up nose. • In one continuous motion, lower toddler just under water surface and scoop up to chest. Give hug and praise. • Repeat skill only once during any given lesson until toddler is comfortable, i.e., no crying, coughing, or choking. • Once the child is comfortable, skill may be repeated up to 3 times in any lesson. 4. Opening eyes— • Have toddler hold up fingers underwater and parent/instructor counts fingers. • Reverse roles and have toddler go underwater to count parent's fingers. Toddler may have to hold parent's arm or side of pool at first.	Breath control

Skill (Positions)	Teaching Notes	Results
G. Back Float (Cheek-to-Cheek: Sandwich; Back Support) (Neck and Back)	1. Adjustment to water in back position— • Parent lowers shoulders into water. • Toddler rests head on parent's shoulder. • Parent talks, hums. • Toddler's legs remain still. • Parent remains motionless or slowly moves backward. 2. Back float readiness— • Parent talks to toddler. Have toddler look into parent's eyes while parent moves backward. *Safety hint:* Parent must watch toddler's face constantly. Avoid moving into other parents and toddlers.	Safety and relaxation

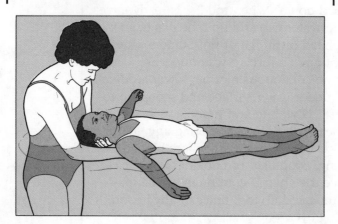

Skill (Positions)	Teaching Notes	Results

H. Back Glide (Neck and Back; Chin and Back)

- Toddler stands on bottom of pool facing away from parent.
- Parent supports toddler under back of neck while keeping correct head position and moving backward.
- Toddler holds onto side of pool, then releases the wall and gently glides backward with parent supporting head and back.
- Repeat above, except toddler holds onto side of pool, and parent uses chin and back support position.

Coordination

I. Arm Movement on Back

Demonstrate back glide with "winging" arms (refer to *Swimming and Aquatics Safety* [SAS] [Stock No. 321133]).

- Parent holds toddler while instructor moves toddler's arms and hands in winging motion.

Propulsion readiness

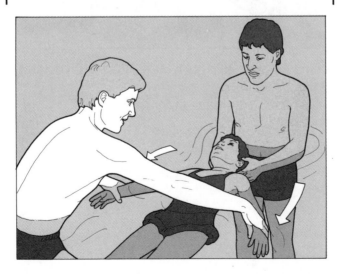

Skill (Positions)	Teaching Notes	Results
J. Combined Skills on Back	• Kick to back glide with support from parent or instructor. • Repeat, using kickboard. • Add winging to kick with support from parent.	Coordination
K. Arm Movement, Prone Position (Arm Stroke; Side-to-Side)	• Parent guides toddler's arms, using cue such as "reach," "paddle," "dig," etc. • Parent or instructor demonstrates beginner arm stroke to toddler. • Toddler imitates arm movement with assistance while sitting on parent's knee. • Toddler practices arm movement independently.	Beginner stroke readiness Propulsion

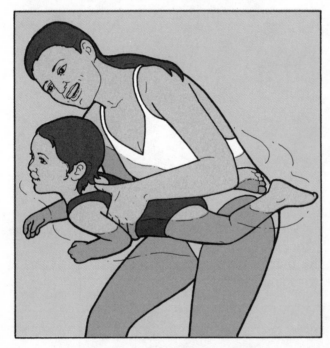

Skill (Positions)	Teaching Notes	Results
L. Combined Skills, Prone Position (Side-to-Side)	• Toddler combines two skills such as arms, kicking, or bubbles. • Parent walks forward so water supports the toddler's body.	Coordination

Skill (Positions)	Teaching Notes	Results

M. Rolling Over	1. Rolling back to front—
	  • Parent holds toddler in cheek-to-cheek: sandwich position.
	  • Parent cues toddler and rotates hands while rolling toddler onto stomach with head up.
	  • Parent's hands move to hold toddler in face-to-face position.
	  • Toddler's head is up when first learning this skill.
	2. Rolling front to back—
	  • Toddler is in face-to-face position. Parent reaches directly across and grasps toddler's upper arm, thumb down, fingers on top.
	  • Fingers of the other hand hold toddler under the armpit and chest, while the thumb (up) holds the upper arm.
	  • While moving backward, parent cues toddler to roll over.
	  • Parent rolls toddler onto back, cueing toddler to look into parent's eyes.
	  • Parent moves hands to neck and back position.
		Safety

N. Personal Flotation Device (PFD)	• Toddler and parent practice putting on PFDs correctly. • Parent may support toddler in PFD. • Toddler rolls over onto back in PFD. • Toddler rolls back over onto front and returns to the wall. • Toddler jumps into water wearing PFD and returns to the wall using beginner arm stroke. • Toddler may wear lightweight clothes under PFD (e.g., T-shirt and shorts; no jeans or sweat shirts/pants) and float in water (limit this activity to a few minutes).	Safety

- Toddler and parent practice "Help" and "Huddle" positions (refer to SAS text for description).

Safety hint: Check PFD for Coast Guard specifications and proper fit to individual toddler.

O. Changing Positions

1. Vertical to prone position—
   - Toddler sits on parent's knee facing, and just beyond reach of, the wall.
   - Parent cues toddler to move toward wall.
   - Parent guides toddler into horizontal position and helps toddler grasp wall.

Body control

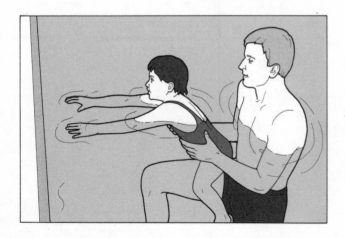

2. Vertical to back float position—
    - Toddler faces away from parent, holding side of pool or standing.
    - Parent supports toddler's shoulders under armpits or chin and back.
    - Parent cues toddler to look up and back at parent's eyes.
    - Parent steps backward, allowing toddler's feet to rise toward surface.

Safety hint: Don't allow toddler's head to submerge.

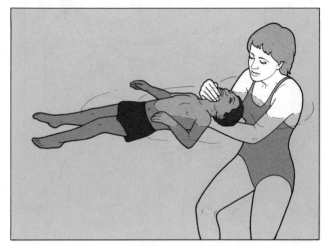

Skill (Positions)	Teaching Notes	Results

P. Kickup

- Using cues, parent remains above water and lowers toddler just below water surface.
- Parent releases toddler briefly and lets toddler kick to surface.
- Parent assists toddler to surface if necessary.
- Parent cues toddler to go underwater independently.

Safety preparation for deep water

Independence and movement

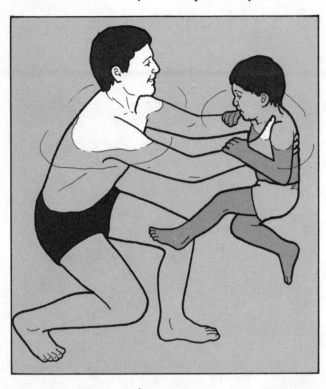 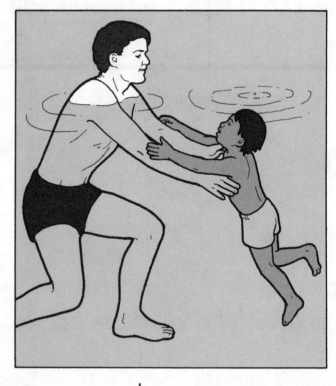

Q. Parent Safety

- Parent practices basic safety skills: reaching, extension, throwing, and wading assists to other parents and toddlers.

Safety awareness

Skill (Positions)	Teaching Notes	Results

- Parents and toddlers should experience wearing PFDs, if appropriate sizes are available.
- Parent wears PFD and practices support and tow of toddler.
- Parent practices elementary forms of rescue on the toddler.

R. Water Exit

- Toddler pulls self out of pool with parent's supervision.
- Toddler uses ladder and stairs where applicable.

Safety hint: Watch for toddlers slipping on steps or stairs or running away from parent.

Independence
Safety

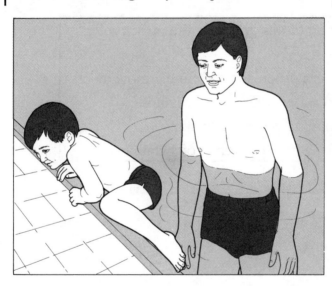

Preschool Skill Progression
(3 to 6 years old)

The Preschool level of this program incorporates the Infant and Toddler level skills and introduces more complex and combination skills. Beginning at this level, most classes will be offered without requiring parental accompaniment in the water.

The instructor is challenged to deal with the wide variety of individual differences at this level, due to variations in age and experience. In addition, without parents in the water accompanying their children, alternative teaching methods need to be considered.

Objectives

As a result of participation in this program, the preschooler will:

- Experience independent propulsive swimming movements.
- Experience advanced water adjustment activities.
- Be exposed to appropriate water safety skills.
- Practice combined skills for basic forms of swimming.

Skill (Positions)	Teaching Notes	Results
A. Water Adjustment (Dance; Hug; Side-to-Face)	1. Getting wet— • Child sits on deck and gets wet using tub toys, washcloths, etc. • Child kicks water at edge of pool. 2. Getting in water— • Child enters water unassisted using ramp, steps, or ladder, or slides in from side of pool. 3. Exploring pool— • Child "walks" hand over hand (on side of pool or gutter) around inside rim of pool.	Readiness Awareness of surroundings
B. Water Entry	Jumping in— • Child jumps to instructor by self, turns around; pushes off bottom to return to the wall in prone glide, with assistance. • Child jumps and returns to wall without assistance.	Safety Independence Self-help
C. Front Kick	• As a group, all children kick while holding onto the edge. • With instructor's assistance, child learns proper use of kickboard and barbells. • Child stands on bottom of pool and blows bubbles while holding kickboard or barbells. • Child kicks with kickboard or barbells with assistance. • Child practices recovery from prone position with assistance (refer to SAS text). • Child kicks with no flotation aid. *Safety hint:* Instructor provides support to opposite end of kickboard or holds barbells steady.	Streamlining body Body control Breath control Movement Independence

Skill (Positions)	Teaching Notes	Results

D. Breath Control

1. Rhythmic bobbing—
   - Child holds onto support and submerges.
   - Child holds onto support, submerges, and blows bubbles.
   - Child repeats submersion rhythmically.

   Safety hint: Watch children to make sure that they keep blowing bubbles, and that they get sufficient air.

2. Rotary breathing—
   - Child holds edge of pool and turns head to one side while blowing bubbles.

Endurance

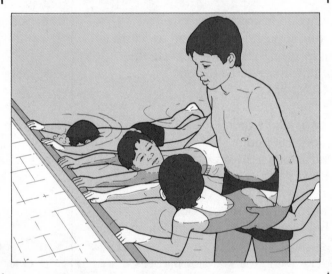

E. Prone Glide

- Instructor helps child glide to wall and secures child's hands to wall.
- Instructor glides child to aide.

Safety hint: Keep distance from instructor to wall at $1\frac{1}{2}$ to 2 body lengths maximum.

Independent movement

- Child pushes off wall to instructor; instructor returns child to wall.
- Child using flotation device pushes off the bottom of pool and glides increasingly longer distances to instructor.
- Child pushes off wall and glides to instructor unassisted.

Safety hint: Instructor must remain within easy reach of all students.

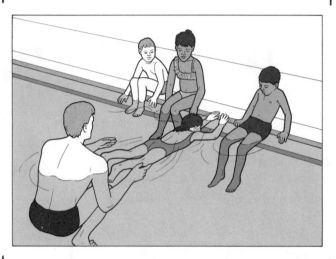

F. Prone Float
- Child pushes off from bottom of pool with little forward motion until motionless. Child holds float for up to 5 seconds.

Buoyancy

G. Underwater Exploration
- Child practices submerging face with instructor's assistance or alone with instructor's cue. Discourage child from wiping eyes.
- Child submerges and opens eyes to grasp object or count fingers.
- Child dives for rings or weighted objects.

Breath control

Skill (Positions)	Teaching Notes	Results
H. Back Float and Recovery (Chin and Back Support)	• Instructor cradles child's chin with one hand. With other hand, instructor supports child's back; cue child to look back into instructor's eyes. • Child practices back float with assisted recovery (see SAS text). • Repeat with unassisted recovery.	Independence Self-confidence Safety

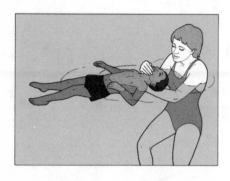  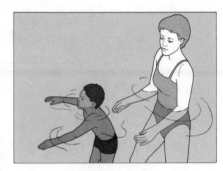

Skill (Positions)	Teaching Notes	Results
I. Combined Stroke on Back (Chin and Back, Neck and Back Support)	• Child practices assisted back glide by pushing off side of pool, with winging (see SAS text). • Practice these skills using flotation devices. • Child practices back glide with winging and flutter kick.	Movement
J. Beginner Stroke, Prone Position (Side-to-Side)	1. Arm movement— • Child practices beginner arm stroke movement (refer to SAS text) with instructor's assistance. 2. Arms and rhythmic breathing— • Child practices arm movement with any breathing pattern. • Child practices drafting with arm movement. Lift chin for breathing.	Strength Coordination Breath control

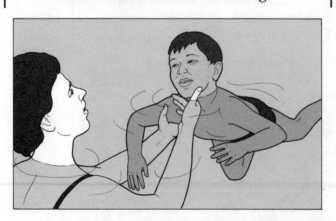

- Repeat arm movement with modified rhythmic breathing but no assistance.
- Repeat arm movement with breathing and no assistance.

3. Arms and rotary breathing—
   - In side-to-side position, instructor supports the child's head with one hand and, with the other hand (side the child is on), manipulates breathing arm.
   - While moving forward, tell child to "Breathe, roll, and blow" (take a breath, roll head into water, and blow bubbles). Repeat.

Coordination
Propulsion

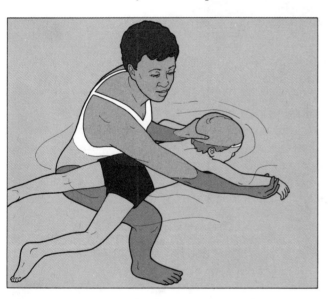
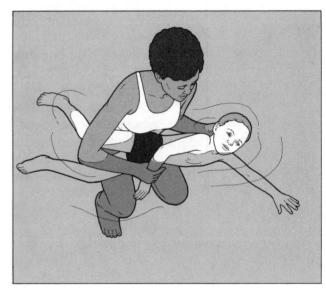

4. Arms, breathing, and kick—
   - Child practices arm and leg movements, and breathing with flotation aid (kickboard, barbell, styrofoam float, etc.).
   - Child attempts beginner stroke arm movement with instructor support.
   - Child practices arm and leg movements and breathing unassisted.

Propulsion

Skill (Positions)	Teaching Notes	Results
K. Rolling Over	1. Rolling front to back— • Instructor faces child. • From prone glide, give cue by tapping back of head, then with the same hand support back of head during roll. • With other hand reach across and grasp child's wrist to help turn the child onto his or her back. • Cue the child to look into instructor's eyes as he or she turns. • Child may need to kick a little to keep legs from dropping. 2. Rolling back to front— • From back glide, instructor reaches across child's stomach and chest to grasp child's wrist. • Instructor's other hand supports back of child's head. Cue child to look into instructor's eyes. • Give verbal cue and pull child's arm across his or her chest to assist with roll. 3. Unassisted roll— • Instructor stands facing child. As child glides toward instructor, cue child by tapping head to initiate roll.	Safety Independence

Skill (Positions)	Teaching Notes	Results
L. Changing Direction	• Child pushes off side of pool, swims around instructor, and returns to wall.	Safety

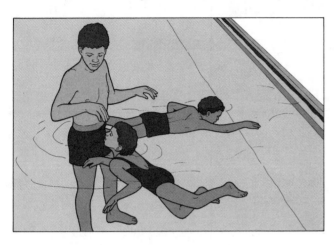 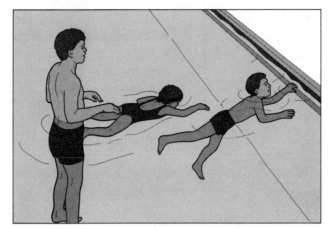

Skill (Positions)	Teaching Notes	Results
M. Bobbing to Safety	• Child bounces up and down off bottom in waist depth toward side of pool. • Gradually increase depth, submerging head, and exhaling underwater.	Safety
N. Kickup	• Child is held under armpits. On cue, child submerges assisted by instructor and kicks feet to the surface. • Starting in the water, child practices unassisted. • Child jumps in and practices kickup with and without assistance from instructor.	Safety preparation for deep water
O. Treading Water	Refer to SAS text.	Safety
P. Personal Flotation Device (PFD)	• Child practices putting on PFDs correctly. • Instructor may support child in PFD. • Child rolls over onto back in PFD. • Child rolls back over on to front and returns to the wall. • Child jumps into water wearing PFD and returns to the wall using beginner arm stroke. • Child may wear lightweight clothes under PFD (e.g., T-shirt and shorts; no jeans or sweat shirts/pants) and float in water (limit this activity to a few minutes). • Child practices "Help" and "Huddle" positions (Refer to SAS text for description). • Child moves in water on front and back with PFD, assisted by instructor. • Repeat with no assistance. *Safety hint:* Check PFD for Coast Guard specifications and proper fit to individual child.	Safety Propulsion Independence

Skill (Positions)	Teaching Notes	Results
Q. Combined Safety Skills	1. Jumping in and rolling over— • Child jumps and begins to swim to instructor, rolls over with assistance, and continues to instructor. • Repeat with no assistance. • Repeat in different water depths. 2. Jumping in and changing direction— • Child jumps in, swims around instructor, and returns to wall. Child may roll over and rest on back at any time. • Practice without assistance.	Safety Propulsion
R. Forms of Rescue	• Child practices rescues (reach, throw) with instructor, using various, available equipment. *Safety hint:* Elementary rescues using body contact are not appropriate at this age.	Safety
S. Rescue Breathing	• Instructor demonstrates rescue breathing to child (refer to *American Red Cross: Standard First Aid* Workbook [Stock No. 329380] for current techniques). Demonstrate, using infant and child manikins if available.	Safety awareness

Teaching Aids

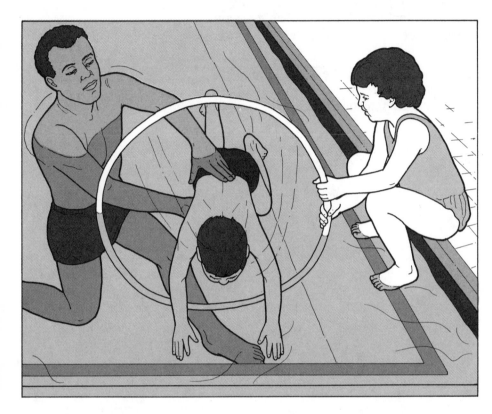

Flotation devices and toys are valuable teaching aids when used skillfully and creatively in the American Red Cross Infant and Preschool Aquatic Program. They can add enjoyment and excitement to the learning experience, as well as facilitating practice of specific skills.

The greatest advantage of teaching aids is that they are fun to use. Instructors can use toys as "icebreakers," and children can bring their favorite toys from home to add familiarity to the new environment. Thus, toys often entice children to try skills that they would not attempt otherwise.

Flotation devices can help provide isolated practice of specific skills. Although these devices can be valuable in assisting young children's aquatic learning, they cannot be a total substitute for one's flotation abilities. They are not to be used as a substitute for good teaching or learning activities; their value is as teaching aids for specific skills and activities as well as initial confidence builders.

Parental supervision cannot be lessened because of the use of flotation devices. Children may become dependent on the use of a flotation device and inappropriately attempt skills that they cannot do without the device. The young child may not realize who or what is helping him or her stay afloat. Young children also may express a degree of attachment to the flotation device that actually impairs their progress.

Following is information about flotation equipment and toys that are commonly used and easily available. Also included are the advantages and disadvantages of each, which item can be used with each skill, proper use (how to hold), and safety guidelines.

Safety hint: Do not leave teaching aids in or near the water when class is not in session. They may lure the child back to the water. Remind parents that this rule applies during water-related activities at home as well.

Kickboards

Advantages
- Provides opportunity for group practice.
- Develops self-confidence.
- Assists in building child's strength and endurance.
- Provides support for practicing positions such as prone float or back float.
- Helps keep face above water during kicking practice.
- Can cut old kickboards in two pieces for smaller children.

Disadvantages
- Children try to climb up on them rather than stretch out.
- Board may slip out of the child's grasp or flip over.

Skill	How to Hold	Safety Guidelines
• Pool exploration	In the side-by-side position, place infant or toddler on the kickboard on the stomach, hands at top of board. With one hand, parent holds far side of board against hip. The other arm holds child's hands on board.	
• Prone float	Hold kickboard in front with arms stretched straight. Hands hold end of board; arms do not rest on board.	When child begins to use board independently, parents and instructor must stay within arm's reach of child.
• Front kick	Hold kickboard in front with arms stretched straight over board. Hands hold top of board so arms rest on board.	
• Back kick	Stage 1: Hold kickboard across stomach. Hands hold far side of board, arms across board. Stage 2: Hold kickboard in water behind and above head, arms stretched straight above head.	Keep board flat on stomach. Use when child has good control of body position.
• Arms and breathing combined, prone position	One hand grasps end of board, arm straight, while other arm pulls.	
• Kicking and breathing combined, prone position	Stage 1: Hold end of board in front with arms stretched straight. Stage 2: Hold board with hand on nonbreathing side. Arm on breathing side rests on child's hip/thigh.	

Personal Flotation Devices (PFDs)

Coast Guard-approved personal flotation devices (PFDs) are designed to keep a person at the surface of the water. For the purposes of this manual, PFDs refer to life jackets only, although there are other types of PFDs. PFDs are particularly recommended for children with certain physical disabilities (see Chapter 2).

Caution parents about depending on PFDs to protect their child against drowning.

Safety hint: The large size of young infants' heads, with their short trunk and legs, makes infants top-heavy and liable to invert in the water when wearing a PFD. Be very cautious when you teach parents the use of PFDs with older infants.

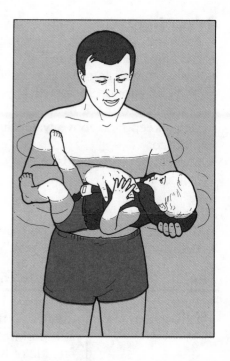

Advantages
- Promotes water relaxation.
- Builds confidence.
- Provides opportunity for group practice.
- Permits child to move independently and frees parent or instructor's hands to assist leg movements.
- Assists in coordination of combined skills.

Disadvantages
- An infant or young child can become inverted in the water if the PFD is too large.
- A panicked infant or young child's movements may cause him or her to float face down.
- Use may foster dependency by child or parent.
- PFD can promote poor body position.
- PFD's bulk reduces effectiveness in performing certain skills.

Skill	How to Hold	Safety Guidelines
• Back float • Back kick • Combined skills: winging and kicking • Elementary back stroke • Treading water	Attach securely: tied and fastened correctly.	During early learning stages, parents and instructor must stay close to child in case of panic or face submersion.
• Front kick	The PFD is not worn on child's body, rather, child holds PFD under chin and chest.	

Barbells

Advantages
- Available in different sizes and materials (wood and styrofoam or plastic and foam), enabling the instructor to use the barbell appropriate to the developmental level or size of the child.
- Easy to make with inexpensive, readily available materials, such as broomsticks, gallon jugs, and silicone sealer.
- Develops self-confidence.
- Assists in building child's strength and endurance.
- Provides support for practicing positions such as prone float or back float.
- Helps keep face above water during kicking practice.

Disadvantages
- May roll out from under child's arms.
- May slip out of child's grasp.
- Can promote poor body position.

Skill	How to Hold	Safety Guidelines
• Prone float • Prone kick	Hold barbell in front with arms stretched straight.	During the early learning stages, parent or instructor must stay within arm's reach of the child in the event they let go, or lose grasp of, the barbell.
• Back float • Back kick	Hold barbell across stomach with arms stretched out straight toward feet.	
• Arm movement	Hold barbell under armpits.	
• Arm and breathing combined	One hand grasps barbell while other arm is pulling.	
• Kicking and breathing combined	Hold barbell in front with arms stretched straight.	
• Treading water	Hold two barbells, one in each hand, out to side.	

Inflatable Arm Bands ("muscles," "wings," "swimmies")

Advantages
- Keeps child's head above the water surface.
- Helps build child's strength and endurance.
- Permits child to move independently and frees parent or instructor's hands to assist with leg movements, to tow, or roll the child over.
- Inflation can gradually be reduced as child's kicking efficiency improves. Some arm bands have pockets that inflate in sections.

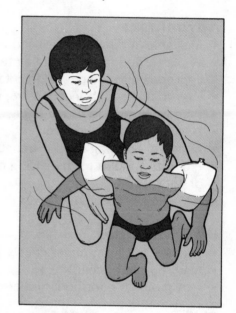

Disadvantages
- May encourage child to overestimate ability.
- May foster dependency by child or parent.
- Tends to slip off.
- May develop leaks at seams or valves.
- Raises child's center of buoyancy, which forces the body into a vertical position.
- May impair a child's progress if he or she has become accustomed to kicking in a vertical position.

Skill	How to Hold	Safety Guidelines
• Kicking • Rolling over • Treading water	Place around upper arms.	Parents and instructors must stay within arm's reach of the child in the event bands slip off or develop a leak.

102

Styrofoam Floats
(cubes, belts, etc., which attach to body)

Advantages
- Promotes relaxation in the water.
- Builds confidence.
- Helps build child's strength and endurance.
- Provides opportunity for group practice.
- Permits child to move independently and frees parent or instructor's hands to assist leg or arm movement.
- Assists in coordination of combined skills.

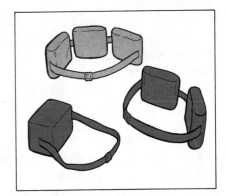

Disadvantages
- May encourage child to overestimate ability.
- May foster dependency by child or parent.
- Can promote poor body position.
- Can submerge child's face if placed too low on an infant or toddler's back.

Skill	How to Hold	Safety Guidelines
• Back float • Combined kicking and winging, back position	Attach so that float lies on the stomach.	During early learning stages, parents and instructors must stay close to child in case the child's face is submerged.
• Combined skills in prone position—arms, kicks, bubbles, or rhythmic breathing	Attach so that float lies on the back.	

Inner Tubes (pull tubes)

Advantages
- Promotes relaxation in the water.
- Maintains child's head above water surface.
- Permits child to move independently and frees the parent or instructor's hands to assist leg movements.
- Provides opportunity for group practice.
- Helps build child's strength and endurance.

Disadvantages
- May develop leaks at seams or valves.
- A child could slip through it.
- May cause irritation if valve stem rubs against child's body. (Use stemless tubes such as pull tubes, or tape in the stem.)
- May foster dependency by child or parent.
- May promote poor body position.
- May impair progress if child becomes accustomed to kicking in a vertical position.

Skill	How to Hold	Safety Guidelines
• Kicking • Treading water	Use under armpits, with arms over tube.	Parents and instructors must stay within arm's reach in case of a leak, or if the child slips through.

Toys

When selecting toys, consider whether they are—
— Safe and appropriate for child's developmental level.
— Too large to be swallowed.
— Durable, as some toys contaminate the water if broken.
— Washable and mildew resistant. (All toys should be disinfected on a regular basis.)
— Colorful and appealing.

Provide enough toys for all participants. Some types of equipment and toys that can add to the fun and success of the course include:

- Balls
- Boats
- Dolls
- Painted shells
- Weighted diving objects
- Plastic fruit/flowers
- Funnels
- Rubber animals
- Sponges
- Brass bells
- Washcloths
- Plastic musical instruments
- Watering cans and buckets
- Hula hoops
- Floating letters/numbers
- Ping pong balls

Safety hint: Keep items stored out of children's sight and reach when not in use.

Skill or Uses	Toys
• Icebreakers	All the above toys and equipment.
• Water adjustment— water on face and head	Sponges, washcloths, watering cans, buckets, and plastic cups.
• Bubbles • Breath control	Ping pong balls (blow them over the water), weighted diving objects, funnels.
• Prone arm and leg movements: "Chase the toy"	All floating toys.
• Prone glide	Hula hoop.
• Underwater exploration (open eyes underwater)	Weighted diving objects.
• Back float (used to distract uneasy child and promote relaxation)	Any toy that can be held.
• Demonstration either by instructor or child (If child is not ready to try a skill he or she can "teach" a doll the skill. This will assist the child's readiness.)	Doll.

7 Images, Games, Songs, and Rhymes

Much of a child's early learning takes place while playing games. In fact, play and fun experiences are essential for the development of a child's positive attitude toward the world. Images, games, and rhymes make use of a child's natural ability to imagine and pretend while learning swimming-related skills.

Images

Young children have very lively imaginations and like to pretend. Give a child a box to play with and it becomes a house, car, bus, train, plane, animal cage, gift, and more. The use of images, or thinking of imaginary objects and activities, utilizes this natural ability and can enhance a young child's willingness to participate and enjoy aquatic activities.

To be successful, images should be:
- Simple and concrete.
- Something from the child's experience.
- Amusing or interesting.
- Able to actively engage the child in movement or participation.

The purpose of the following is to give you examples of how to encourage children to use images to learn.

Water Adjustment
- Kneel at edge of pool like a frog to blow bubbles.
- Spill water out of containers to make waterfalls.
- Move hands in and out of the water like a porpoise jumping in the waves.
- "Paint" the child's body and then wash off the paint.

Kicking
- Use a kickboard to kick and be a motor boat.
- Have a horse race; see who finishes first. Children say "giddy-up" as they kick across the pool.
- Be a whale; kick in the back float position. The feet become the whale's tail.
- Kick to become a water fountain. How low or high can the water go?

Back Float
- Be a leaf floating on a pond.
- Float like a boat or a log.
- Be an airplane or a butterfly and stretch out your wings (arms).
- Pretend it's nighttime and quietly count the stars (lights).

Underwater Exploration
- Be a submarine; listen to the sounds while blowing bubbles underwater.
- Pretend to be a seed. Go under the water and spread out your leaves or flowers (arms) when you surface.

Arm Stroke
- Be a puppet: the instructor patterns the child's arms.
- Swim with spoons (keep fingers together). Spreading fingers or using forks are incorrect positions.
- Be a dog burying her bones by "digging in" with "big paws."

Prone Float
- Be a rocket ship with arms overhead, and carefully blast off across the pool.
- With hands overhead, make long bunny ears.
- Pretend to be Superman flying through the air.
- Stretch out arms and legs to be a big fish in the water.

Combination Skills
- Be a dog burying bones and growling to keep people away: look (turn head to side to breathe) and growl (place head in water and blow bubbles).
- Pretend to be a parachute jumper. Jump in the water, turn, level off, and return to the edge of the pool.
- Be a favorite circus animal and do the beginner stroke (no breathing) through a hoop to a stationary support.

Games and Songs for Skill Development

Games are associated with fun, but they provide for the development of these critical skills:
- Motor skills—Coordination, balance, gross and fine motor control, and spatial awareness.
- Survival skills—Personal water safety skills as well as general water safety knowledge.
- Social skills—Interaction, cooperation, and leadership.

Games and other activities must be chosen with care. They need to *be appropriate to the level of ability of participants, help ensure safety,* and *provide enjoyment* as well.

Games and activities can be *educational* or *recreational* in nature. They can be selected to teach new skills or practice skills already mastered.

When choosing games, consider the following three concerns:

1. Purpose: Know the aim of the game or activity.
2. Safety: Most activities can be made safe and suitable by adding rules or modifying the game. However, forethought and planning are necessary.
3. Equipment: Prior to the lesson, organize special equipment required for the game.

The games which follow are listed by the appropriate water-related skill and/or activity to be taught. Accompanying song lyrics can be found at the end of this chapter. Some appropriate rhymes are also reprinted for possible use during classes.

WATER ADJUSTMENT

Game or Song	Description	Adaptation
Birthday Party	Have an imaginary party in the pool. Blow bubbles (candles), sing songs, and get presents underwater.	
Piggyback Ride	Parent or instructor backs up against side of pool. Child hops on adult's back, putting arms loosely around neck. Adult then proceeds across pool—stooping with straight back—while child kicks feet.	Ride lying on kickboards.
Motor Boat	Form large circle. Parent holds child in float position on outside of circle. Start engine by blowing bubbles. Speed up, slow down, and put on brakes by leaning back into back float position.	Tow child by hands or support under arms.
"Pop Goes the Weasel"	Form circle. Parent can hold child. Move to right or left, singing song. At the end of each verse, parent raises child up in the air and lowers him or her to shoulders.	
Simon Says	Tell class to do any skill that you are practicing if you say, "Simon Says." If they don't hear "Simon Says," they don't move.	Use variety of skills: kicking, arms, bubbles, etc.
"Wheels on the Bus"	Parent is in shallow water, child is in dance position, slowly bouncing in a circle. Windows: bob up and down. Wiper: hold under armpits facing child, and move from side to side. Horn: slap the water.	
"Down by the Station"	Child grabs edge of pool and pulls self along gutter, pretending arms are the train wheels. Parent should be next to or behind child for safety. Follow the leader who is the engine; end is the caboose.	Blow underwater on "toot toot." Explore the pool lights, ladders, water outlets. Make tunnels.
"Mulberry Bush"	Hold hands in circle, or do as a warm-up while children sit on edge of pool. Follow the directions in the song: wash face, ears, hair, etc.	If child can't stand, parent holds child in front as they form a circle. Substitute swim terms in the song.

Game or Song	Description	Adaptation
Water Exercises	Exercises are good for balance, loosening up, and staying warm, e.g., jumping jacks, running forward/backward, hopping, skipping, and arm circles.	Some exercises can be performed with parent holding the child.
Finger Counting	Paired groups take turns counting each other's fingers underwater.	Face or entire body can be submerged to count fingers.
Blow the Cork	Children take turns blowing the cork to each other or as members of a team during relay races.	Balloons and/or ping pong balls can also be used.
I Spy	Children identify objects placed underwater by size, color, or shape.	Objects can be spotted with or without submerging and can be picked up and given to instructor or parent.
"London Bridge"	Bridge can be made with arms and legs, holding kickboards, etc. Go through bridge in different ways.	Parent holds child. Preschooler is unassisted.
Follow the Leader	Instructor is the first leader and does a skill which everyone else imitates, e.g., jump, bubbles, or kick. Take turns being leader.	
Talk to Feet	Child talks to feet by blowing bubbles, turns head to one side, listens to what they say.	Talk to hands.
Retrieve the Balls (Corks)	Starting at one side of pool, children retrieve balls or corks floating on other side of pool. Child with most collected at end of game wins.	Parent may hold child.
"Hokey Pokey"	Stand in circle and imitate words of song.	
"Did You Ever See a Lassie?"	Form a circle. Parent holds child at side. Gently glide child forward on stomach and backward on back as group sings. Repeat verse with "laddie."	
Water Push Ball	Form a circle. Instructor places ball in center. Children try to move ball by splashing and pushing water with their hands, or by kicking from back float position.	Divide into buddy pairs. Push ball back and forth. Parent holds child and assists.

Game or Song	Description	Adaptation
"It's Raining, It's Pouring"	Dribble, drop, and splash water over heads with sponges, cups, etc.	Take game into the shower. Child makes "rain" on instructor or parent.
"If You're Happy and You Know It"	Sing song and follow along with words. Parent assists child with motions.	
Choo-Choo Train	Become a train; make train noises. Travel around and discover ladders, lights, water outlets, etc. Go through tunnels made by instructor, who places hands on edge of pool and arches with body.	Parent assists child in movement around pool.
Play Buddies	Children are paired. Instructor leads play: turn to your buddy and shake hands, join hands and skip in a circle, clap hands, hold hands and blow bubbles.	Vary activities according to skill level. Parent and child can be buddies.

WATER ENTRY

Game or Song	Description	Adaptation
Hoop Jumping	Standing at the edge, child jumps into the hoop.	Assist child. Practice at varying depths.
"Humpty Dumpty"	Child falls or jumps in from sitting or standing position.	Assist child. Vary depths.
"Jack"	Child jumps in when his or her name is called.	Assist child. Child jumps in over out-stretched arm or pole.
Children in the Pool (Tune of "Farmer in the Dell")	Repeat following using each child's name: "Mary's in the pool, oh Mary's in the pool." Children can enter as instructed, or as they wish.	Assist child. Vary depths.
Imagination	Enter the pool like crocodiles, marching soldiers, ducks with flapping wings, or doing the elephant walk.	Follow the leader. Vary entry point, depth, and leader.

SUBMERGING

Game or Song	Description	Adaptation
Treasure Hunt	Various objects are retrieved from bottom of pool. Keeping eyes open will make task easier.	Size of objects and depth of location will vary according to swimming ability.
Submarine	At signal from the "Captain," children submerge. The "submarine" under longest becomes the next "Captain."	Either face or entire head can be submerged.
"London Bridge"	(see page 111)	
Longfellow the Whale	Children, in a circle, attempt to exhale when submerging. The child who is most successful becomes "Longfellow of the Week."	Face or entire head in water while blowing bubbles.
Fireman's Pole	Children in deep water go down a rescue pole (encourage submerging before returning to surface).	Preschool only.
Water Dodge Ball	In a circle, play a game of dodge ball with a soft plastic ball. Children dodge the ball by ducking underwater.	Face or entire head in water while blowing bubbles. Parent can hold child.
Disappearing Fish Game	Standing in a circle with the "It" person in the middle, each child attempts to disappear under the water before being tagged.	Child must submerge in order to play game.
Ring Around the Rosie	Form circle, holding hands. Alternate adult-child-adult. Submerge on "We all fall down."	
Buddy Bobbing (See Saw)	Buddy pairs hold hands. One buddy goes right under and comes up. The other buddy does the same.	Parent and child can be buddies. Vary depth. Change partners.
Baby Dolphin	Instructor places the "baby" through a hoop into outstretched hands of parent.	Eliminate the hoop.
Washing Machine	Parent pretends to put soap on child's hair and scrub it clean. To rinse soap off, tip head to right side, then left side; tip head back; put head partially under; submerge head.	Submerge head right away.

Game or Song	Description	Adaptation
Tea Party or Picnic	Invite children and parents to a tea party. Describe what you will be serving. Sit on the bottom and have a party.	Hold the tea party on steps. Some children are above the water while others are under the water. Preschoolers can set table, put food on table, all go eat, and clean up.
The Best Log	Instructor counts while children do back float.	Child can be supported by parent or use a kickboard.

FLOTATION

Game or Song	Description	Adaptation
Battleship	Position of ship at port is explained as being on back, looking for airplanes. Ship leaves port and starts engines by kicking.	Child can be supported by parent or use a kickboard.
"Twinkle, Twinkle"	Children are on backs with arms and legs outstretched. Parent sings "Twinkle, Twinkle, Little Star" softly in child's ear.	Child can be supported.
Imagination	Be a leaf floating on a pond; float like a cork; be a butterfly and stretch out arms or wings; pretend it's nighttime and count the stars.	Child can be supported.
Merry-Go-Round	Circle all holding hands. Number off in twos (horses and camels, bees and butterflies, etc.). Walk around circle in same direction. On signal, ones float on their back/front supported by twos. Ready, Go—reverse direction and call out twos. Ones lend support.	Put parents between each child for support.
Imagination (Rocket Ship)	Carefully blast off across the pool as a torpedo, rocket ship, etc.	Use kickboards or parent for support.

ROLLING OVER

Game or Song	Description	Adaptation
Row, Row, Row-Your-Boat	While singing, parent gently turns child from front to back to front. Use gliding movements.	Assist child in activity. Start on front and call out "over easy."
"I'm a Little Pancake"	Parents hold "pancakes" on back, walking backward. When singing "flip me over," roll child to front. Then vice versa.	Keep child's face out of the water.
Sunbathing	Children do back float, then rotate to front to get well tanned.	Assist child in activity.
Eggs for Breakfast	Children begin in a front float. Instructor calls out "Sunny side up," and children roll over to a back float.	Keep child's face out of the water.

116

KICKING

Game or Song	Description	Adaptation
"London Bridge"	(see page 111)	
Simon Says	(see page 110)	
Red Light–Green Light	Skills are alternately started and stopped by red/green light command.	Bubbles can be started and stopped.
Motor Boat	(see page 110)	
Water Fountain	Form a circle. Back float with feet in center. Kick to see how high the water can go, how low it can go.	Child assisted in floating position.
Water Push Ball	(see page 111)	
Loud and Quiet Kicking	On cue, all children kick loudly (splashing), then switch to quiet kicking (under water's surface).	
Kickboard Races	Children in waves or relay teams use kickboard skills to compete. They pretend to be on horses and say "giddy-up."	Parent holds kickboard for child.

ARM STROKE

Game or Song	Description	Adaptation
Frog in the Sea, You Can't Catch Me	The instructor (frog) runs after the class as they walk and pull through the water. If the "frog" catches the "tadpole," the caught person is the new "frog."	Parent assists child. Walk backward, scooping water forward.
Water Fountain	Form a large circle. Instructor is in center. Children scoop (stroke) into center of circle and touch hand of instructor. Turn on back and kick out (splashing instructor).	Parent assists child. Blow bubbles on way in.
Imagination	Child is a puppet; instructor patterns the child's arms. "Dog" buries bones by "digging in" with "big arms." Make taffy.	

COMBINATION SKILLS

Game or Song	Description	Adaptation
Steal the Fish	Children race for an object on the bottom when their numbers are called. Children kick and/or swim to object underwater and then return to starting point.	Use floating objects. Parents may help child locate object.
Around the Lighthouse	The instructor is the lighthouse. Children are asked to swim around and back to the edge.	Child uses combined front and back skills to swim around the instructor. May be used as a relay.
Flip Flop	Children are on side of pool. Jump in, level off, and begin swim on front. When instructor says "flip," children turn over and swim on back; says "flop," they roll onto their fronts again.	Assist child in skills.
Parachute Jumper	Children jump in the water, turn, level off, and return to edge of pool.	Assist child in skills.

Water Fun 'n' Rhymes

The following rhymes are related to things found in and around water.
The instructor should chant each line, then act out the actions with the
class.

BULLFROG
Here's Mr. Bullfrog
Sitting on a rock.
Along comes a little boy
Mr. Bullfrog jumps—KERPLOP!

LITTLE FROG
A little frog in a pond am I,
Hippity, hippity, hop.
I can jump in the air so high,
HIPPITY, HIPPITY, HOP!

MY TURTLE
This is my turtle
He lives in a shell;
He likes his home very well.
He pokes his head out when he wants to eat
And pulls it back when he wants to sleep.

Songs and Lyrics

"LONDON BRIDGE"
London Bridge is falling down,
Falling down, falling down.
London Bridge is falling down,
My fair lady.

Take a key and lock her up,
Lock her up, lock her up.
Take a key and lock her up,
My fair lady.

Off to prison we must go,
We must go, we must go.
Off to prison we must go,
My fair lady.

"WHEELS ON THE BUS"
The wheels on the bus go
round and round,
round and round, round and round.
The wheels on the bus go
round and round,
All through the town.

The windows on the bus go up and down. . .

The wipers on the bus go swish, swish, swish. . .

The horn on the bus goes beep, beep, beep. . .

The motor on the bus goes (blow bubbles)

"DOWN BY THE STATION"
Down by the station
Early in the morning,
See the little puffer-bellies
All in a row.
See the engine driver
Pull the little handle,
Puff, puff, toot, toot,
Here we go.

"IF YOU'RE HAPPY AND YOU KNOW IT"
If you're happy and you know it
Clap your hands.
If you're happy and you know it
Clap your hands.
If you're happy and you know it
And you really want to show it,
If you're happy and you know it
Clap your hands.

Repeat:
2. Blow bubbles...
3. Wash your hair...
4. Stroke your arms...
5. Kick your feet...
6. Shout "Hooray"...
7. Jump up and down...

"HOKEY POKEY"
You put your right hand in,
You put your right hand out,
You put your right hand in and
You shake it all about. (turn in place)
You do the Hokey Pokey and
You turn yourself around,
That's what it's all about.

Repeat with variations:
Left hand, head, whole self

"PANCAKES" (Tune: "I'm a Little Teapot")
I'm a little pancake on my back,
I'm a little pancake nice and flat.
I'm a little pancake on my back,
Flip me over just like that!

"POP GOES THE WEASEL"
All around the cobbler's bench,
The monkey chased the weasel.
The monkey thought it was all in fun,
POP goes the weasel.

A penny for a spool of thread,
A penny for a needle.
That's the way the money goes,
POP goes the weasel.

"HUMPTY DUMPTY"
Humpty Dumpty sat on a wall
Humpty Dumpty had a great fall
All the king's horses and
All the king's men
Couldn't put Humpty together again.

"JACK"
Jack be nimble, Jack be quick,
Jack jump over the candlestick.

LITTLE TURTLE RHYME

There was a little turtle
He swam in a puddle
He climbed on the rocks
He snapped at a mosquito
He snapped at a flea
He snapped at a minnow
He snapped at me
He caught the mosquito
He caught the flea
He caught the minnow
But he didn't catch me.

LITTLE FISH

Little fish goes out to play
He wiggles his fins
Then swims away,
He swims and swims in the water bright.
He swims and swims both day and night.

HERE WE GO 'ROUND THE MULBERRY BUSH

Here we go 'round the mulberry bush, the mulberry bush,
Here we go 'round the mulberry bush,
Early in the morning (everyone is in a circle).
This is the way we wash our face, wash our face, wash our face,
This is the way we wash our face
Early in the morning.

Repeat:
3. This is the way we kick our feet. . .
4. This is the way we blow some bubbles. . .
5. This is the way we jump up and down. . .
6. This is the way we clap our hands. . .

Glossary

Animistic: Believing that all objects (e.g., teddy bears, dolls, sun, and moon) are alive.

Autonomous: Self-governing, independent.

Behavioral: Pertaining to actions or behavior.

Cognitive: Relating to knowledge or the act of thinking.

Developmental Sequence: An ordered set of changes in behavior.

Discrimination: The ability to recognize differences among things.

Echo-locate: To locate distant or invisible objects by means of reflected sound waves.

Egocentric: Self-centered.

Emergency Action Plan: A method for preparing and responding to an emergency such as at a pool.

Feedback: Information about someone's performance or behavior.

Giardia: An infectious intestinal parasite which causes diarrhea.

Gross Motor Skill: Related to activity involving a large muscle group.

Hyponatremia: A rare condition of sodium imbalance.

Hypothermia: A lowering of the core body temperature due to cold conditions in the environment.

Inanimate: Not alive.

Infant: For the purposes of the American Red Cross Infant and Preschool Aquatic Program, a young child between 6 and 18 months of age.

Knowledge of Performance: Information about how a person moves his or her body (movement pattern, arm movements, etc.).

Knowledge of Results: Information about what resulted from a person's movement (the distance, height, length of time achieved, etc.).

Learning Style: Characteristic way a person prefers to learn, such as through seeing, hearing, or doing.

Locomotor: Related to the act of moving from place to place. Can refer to movement on land or in the water.

Preschooler: For the purposes of the American Red Cross Infant and Preschool Aquatic Program, a young child 3 through 5 years of age.

Prone: Lying in a horizontal position with the front of the body facing down.

Psychomotor: Relating to movements created by the action of human muscles.

Readiness: State of being ready to do something.

Reinforcement: Positive or negative feedback that affects the likelihood of repeating an action or behavior.

Rhythmic Breathing: A pattern of inhaling and exhaling air, combined with repeated face or head immersion.

Rotary Breathing: A pattern of breathing during swimming involving turning the head to the side to get a breath.

Sensory: Relating to the senses, such as seeing, hearing, or touching.

Separation/Stranger Anxiety: A condition observed in infants who cry when separated from their parents or placed near strangers.

Small Motor Skills: Related to movements by small muscle groups, especially manipulative actions such as writing, drawing, or eating.

Toddler: For the purposes of the American Red Cross Infant and Preschool Aquatic Program, a young child from 18 to 36 months of age.

Tympanostomy: An operation which places a small tube in the eardrum.

Appendixes

APPENDIX A

AQUATIC ACTIVITY PROGRAMS FOR CHILDREN UNDER THE AGE OF THREE (COUNCIL FOR NATIONAL COOPERATION IN AQUATICS)

1. AQUATIC PROGRAMS FOR CHILDREN UNDER THE AGE OF THREE YEARS, MOST APPROPRIATELY, SHOULD BE PROMOTED, DESCRIBED, AND CONDUCTED AS WATER "ADJUSTMENT," "ORIENTATION," OR "FAMILIARIZATION" PROGRAMS. EMPHASIS SHOULD BE PLACED UPON THE NEED FOR YOUNG CHILDREN TO EXPLORE THE AQUATIC ENVIRONMENT IN ENJOYABLE, NON-STRESSFUL SITUATIONS THAT PROVIDE A WIDE VARIETY OF GAMES AND EXPERIENCES.

    RATIONALE: Other terms, such as "drownproofing," "waterproofing," and "water safe," often can suggest to parents and the general public that children can be safe in and around the water without careful supervision. In addition, the developmental literature supports the primary role of play activities and movement exploration in the acquisition of movement competence by young children.

2. WATER EXPERIENCE/ORIENTATION PROGRAMS SHOULD HAVE THE IN-WATER PARTICIPATION OF A PARENT, GUARDIAN, OR OTHER PERSON WHO IS RESPONSIBLE FOR AND TRUSTED BY THE CHILD.

    RATIONALE: The parent is the first and primary teacher of the young child. As such, the parent must assume actual responsibility for the supervision and learning of the child. Aquatic programs, when properly structured, can provide an excellent type of parent-child learning environment. Programs conducted without parents in the water should be limited in size, and make every consideration for the safety and psychological comfort of the child.

3. THE PARTICIPATING PARENT, GUARDIAN, OR OTHER RESPONSIBLE ADULT ASSUMES PRIMARY RESPONSIBILITY FOR MONITORING THE CHILD'S HEALTH BEFORE, DURING, AND AFTER PARTICIPATION IN AQUATIC PROGRAMS. ALL CHILDREN, ESPECIALLY THOSE WITH KNOWN MEDICAL PROBLEMS, SHOULD RECEIVE CLEARANCE FROM THEIR PHYSICIAN PRIOR TO PARTICIPATION IN THE AQUATIC PROGRAM.

RATIONALE: The child's parent and physician are the persons who can best judge the child's medical and developmental readiness for exposure to a public swimming pool at an early age. There is disagreement among professionals about the benefits and detriments of the child's early exposure to the aquatic environment. The potential benefits of enhanced movement, socialization, and parent-child interaction must be weighed against problems such as possible increased susceptibility to eye, ear, respiratory, and bacterial infections. More definitive research evidence is needed to assist parents and physicians in evaluating the child's readiness.

4. PERSONNEL DIRECTING AND OPERATING AQUATIC PROGRAMS FOR CHILDREN UNDER THREE YEARS OF AGE SHOULD HAVE TRAINING IN CHILD DEVELOPMENT AND PARENTING AS WELL AS AQUATICS, OR HAVE CONSULTANTS WHO HAVE BEEN TRAINED IN THESE AREAS. FULLY TRAINED AND QUALIFIED LIFEGUARDS MUST BE ON DUTY AT ALL TIMES DURING PROGRAMS.

RATIONALE: Because of the developmental differences in cognitive, psychomotor, and affective domains between the young child and older children, the directors and teachers of these programs must have a well-founded understanding of child development. Because the programs usually involve both the parents and the children, a further understanding of parenting principles also is necessary. Finally, in spite of the presence of parents in the pool, it must be recognized that the instructor cannot assume lifeguarding responsibilities while teaching. A certified lifeguard in addition to the instructor is needed.

5. PARTICIPATION IN AQUATIC PROGRAMS BY NEONATES AND BY YOUNG CHILDREN LACKING PRONE HEAD CONTROL SHOULD BE LIMITED.

RATIONALE: While there is general disagreement among professionals and practitioners regarding the youngest age at which children should begin water experiences, there is some evidence suggesting that until the child can voluntarily control the head by lifting it 90 degrees when prone, they probably will gain little from the water experience, and may be more at risk of accidentally submerging or swallowing water. Certain aquatic skills can successfully be introduced when the child demonstrates rolling over, crawling, and creeping. Due to individual differences among young children, behavioral, rather than strict age, criteria are usually the most valid way to evaluate children for program participation.

6. CERTAIN TEACHING TECHNIQUES, SUCH AS DROPPING A CHILD FROM A HEIGHT, SHOULD BE STRICTLY PROHIBITED. OTHER PROCEDURES SUCH AS FACE SUBMERSIONS, ESPECIALLY THOSE WHICH ARE CONTROLLED BY AN ADULT, MUST BE LIMITED BOTH IN DURATION AND IN NUMBER FOR THE YOUNG CHILD.

RATIONALE: Dropping a child from any height is unnecessary and serves no reasonable purpose. In fact, it is extremely dangerous, as it may produce head, neck, or organ damage to a young child, as well as introduce water and bacteria into the nose, ears, and sinuses. There is also potential for psychological trauma in such an activity.

A growing number of recent clinical reports have implicated the practice of repeated submersions during aquatic programs in producing hyponatremia, or "water intoxication" in young children. Hyponatremia is a condition in which an electrolyte (especially sodium) imbalance results from the loss of electrolytes or rapid ingestion of fluids or both. The symptoms include such "soft" signs as irritability, crying, and fussing, as well as more serious signs of vomiting, convulsions, and coma. Despite claims that a young child has a "breathholding" or epiglottal reflex, both children and adults can swallow significant amounts of water while learning to swim. Due to the small body size and large skin area to body weight ratio of most children under 18 months of age, water ingestion can produce symptoms of hyponatremia, some of which may be going unnoticed by parents and teachers. Therefore, submersions by young children must be brief (one to five seconds), and few in number (less than six per lesson) while the child is initially learning. Once the child can initiate the submersions AND can demonstrate competent breath control, submersions can become longer and more frequent. However, the parents and teachers still must be alert to bloated stomachs and "soft" signs that may indicate excessive water ingestion and incipient problems.

The condition of hyponatremia must be the focus of a concerted research effort to discover the extent and scope of its presence in infant swimming classes. Clinical and empirical evidence should be the basis for subsequent amendments to this guidelines.

7. MAXIMUM IN-WATER CLASS TIME FOR INFANTS AND VERY YOUNG CHILDREN MUST NOT EXCEED 30 MINUTES.

RATIONALE: Most children benefit from shorter, but more frequent, learning experiences. Limiting in-water time to less than 30 minutes should maximize the learning and enjoyment of children while avoiding fatigue, hypothermia and possible hyponatremia.

Once of the constant factors discovered in each clinical hyponatremia case was that children had been in the water far in excess of 30 minutes. Apparently, fatigue, chilling, and excessive submersions all may contribute to hyponatremia.

8. WATER AND AIR TEMPERATURE MUST BE MAINTAINED AT SUFFICIENT LEVELS AND IN PROPER PROPORTION TO ONE ANOTHER TO GUARANTEE THE COMFORT OF YOUNG CHILDREN.

    RATIONALE: Young children can become chilled more easily than adults and may have immature thermal regulatory systems. They also cannot enjoy the experience or learn optimally if chilled. There is no general agreement as to the proper level of water temperature in indoor pools. However, experience suggests that water temperature should be a MINIMUM of 82 degrees Fahrenheit (86 is preferable) and that air temperature should be at least three degrees higher than the water temperature. Locker and changing room temperatures also should be maintained at warm levels. Failure to achieve these minimum standards should be a strong factor in cancelling or shortening classes.

9. ALL LAWS AND REGULATIONS PERTAINING TO WATER PURITY, POOL CARE, AND SANITATION MUST BE CAREFULLY FOLLOWED.

    RATIONALE: Young children are extremely susceptible to diseases. Utmost care in maintaining facilities in accord with bathing codes and water purity standards can prevent unnecessary outbreaks of disease and infections. Locker rooms and pool decks must be clean and free of clutter. Slippery surfaces and impeded walkways can be very dangerous to beginning and inexperienced walkers. Proper facilities for the changing and disposal of diapers and soiled clothing must be provided.

10. APPROPRIATE, BUT NOT EXCESSIVE CLOTHING SHOULD BE WORN BY YOUNG CHILDREN TO MINIMIZE THE SPREAD OF BODY WASTES INTO THE WATER.

    RATIONALE: Fecal matter is aesthetically unattractive and potentially hazardous to other swimmers. Children should wear some type of tight-fitting but lightweight apparel, perhaps covered by rubber pants. Heavier diapers can be both a health and safety hazard and should not be worn. Parents and instructors should monitor young children and remove them from the water if a bowel movement is apparent.

Printed with permission of the Council for National Cooperation in Aquatics, 901 West New York St., Indianapolis, IN 46223

APPENDIX B

SAMPLE ACCIDENT REPORT

PLEASE PRINT

Name of injured _____ Age ____ Sex ____

Address _____ Zip _____

Phone _____

Date and time of injury _____

Person reporting accident _____

How did the accident occur? Ask injured person to explain in his or her own words.

_____

Describe nature of injury _____

_____

Explain first aid given _____

Person giving first aid _____

EMS called? Time _____ Time EMS arrived _____

Services rendered _____

_____

Notification of relatives: Family member (specify) _____

Other_____ Time of notification _____

Action _____

Is injured insured? _____ Type _____

Please give the names and phone numbers of two witnesses:

_____
Witness   Phone

_____
Witness   Phone

Name of person completing report _____ Date _____

Signature _____

Director of facility: _____ Date _____

Upon completion of this report, deliver to the person in charge or to the recreation office.

APPENDIX C

50 WAYS TO SAY "VERY GOOD!"

Specific feedback about what a child has done well will help improve his or her performance the most. When giving praise, remember to be specific, for example: "Super ____(name)____ , you held your breath for 2 seconds!"

1. *Note:* Always try to remember to use the name of the student.
2. _____(name)_____, you're doing a good job!
3. You did a lot of work today, ____(name)____ !
4. Now you've figured it out.
5. That's RIGHT!
6. Now you have the hang of it!
7. You did it great that time!
8. FANTASTIC!
9. TERRIFIC!
10. Good for you!
11. GOOD WORK!
12. That's better.
13. EXCELLENT!
14. That's a good (boy/girl).
15. That's the best you have ever done.
16. Good going!
17. Keep it up!
18. That's really nice.
19. Keep up the good work.
20. Much better!
21. Good for you!
22. SUPER!
23. Nice going.
24. You make it look easy.
25. Way to go!
26. You're getting better every day.
27. WONDERFUL!
28. I knew you could do it.
29. Keep working on it. . . you're getting better.
30. You're really working hard today.
31. That's the way to do it!
32. Keep on trying!
33. You are very good at that.
34. You are learning fast.
35. You certainly did well today.
36. You've just about got it.
37. I'm happy to see you working like that!
38. I'm proud of the way you worked today!
39. That's the right way to do it.
40. MARVELOUS!
41. Now you've figured it out.
42. PERFECT!
43. You figured that out fast.
44. You're really improving.
45. I think you've got it now.
46. You've done a great job, _____(name)_____ !
47. Congratulations, you got (number) right!
48. You can be proud of yourself for not giving up!
49. You can be proud of yourself for doing so well!
50. You've gotten the hardest part right.

APPENDIX D

SAMPLE PROGRAM ORIENTATION FLYER

(Infant and Toddler Levels)

The ___(name of facility/organization)___ is pleased to have you participate in the American Red Cross Infant and Preschool Aquatic Program. You and your child will have an opportunity to experience water play and water safety. The following information will help create a safe, positive experience for you and your child.

CLASS SCHEDULE
- Tuesdays and Thursdays
- 5:30 to 6:00 p.m.
- 30-minute sessions
- June 23–August 4
- 7 weeks

Be on time for class. Allow plenty of time before and after class for showering and dressing. Attend every class, as frequency is the key to learning.

RELATED COURSE RECOMMENDATIONS
American Red Cross CPR: Infant and Child
American Red Cross Standard First Aid
American Red Cross Basic Water Safety
American Red Cross Swimming Classes for Adults

FACILITY RULES AND REGULATIONS
- Park on the east side of the building.
- No shoes are allowed on the pool deck.
- No drinks, food, or gum is allowed in the pool or locker room.
- Diapers should be properly disposed of in the locker room.
- Use plastic bottles or containers in showers.
- Do not use electrical appliances in the locker room.
- No one is allowed to go into the pool area until one of the class instructors is on deck.

CLOTHING
- Jewelry should be removed prior to class.
- Corrective lenses should be worn when necessary.
- Your child must wear cloth diapers and plastic pants with tight-fitting legs.
- Lightweight T–shirts may be worn for warmth.
- Bring two towels for your child—one for the pool area and one for after showering.
- Bring a padlock from home so that you can lock your valuables.

HEALTH

Please tell your instructor if you and/or your child have any medical problems or disabilities such as—
—Diabetes
—Epilepsy
—Cerebral palsy
—Severe diarrhea
—Chronic ear, nose, and throat infections

Food or drink, especially citrus products, should not be consumed for at least one hour before class.

If your child becomes chilled or tired, take your child out of the water, wrap him or her up warmly, and observe the remainder of the class.

PARENT'S ROLE

- Children copy parental attitudes. What you say, do, and your facial expressions will influence your child.
- Praise your child. Reinforce all skills you want your child to repeat. Reward effort as well as accomplishments.
- Be positive. Ignore or minimize negative reactions such as crying and temper tantrums.
- Have patience. Children progress at their own rate in swimming readiness, just as in all other areas of development.

PARENTS ARE RESPONSIBLE AT ALL TIMES FOR THE SAFETY OF THEIR CHILDREN.

We know that this will be a fun and rewarding time for each of you. Do not hesitate to talk to the instructors at any time throughout the program.

APPENDIX E

SAMPLE EMERGENCY MEDICAL INFORMATION

PLEASE PRINT

PARENTS: Please complete the following information and return this sheet to your instructor on the first day of class.

Child's Name _____ Birth Date _____

Age _____ Sex _____

Parent or Guardian _____ Telephone_____
Address _____
City/State_____ ZIP_____
Employer _____ Telephone _____

IF NOT AVAILABLE IN AN EMERGENCY PLEASE NOTIFY:

Name _____ Telephone _____
Address _____
Relationship_____

1. Has child had any serious illness, injury, or operation?
    If yes, give dates and explanation. _____
    _____

2. Will child be taking any medication? If yes, indicate types and effects on child.
    _____

3. Does child have a physical or mental disability about which the instructor needs to be aware for instructional modifications or emergency purposes?
    If yes, please explain. _____
    _____

APPENDIX F

SAMPLE LESSON PLANS
(First 2 Lessons at each Level)

Infant Level

Time: Maximum 30 minutes in the water.

Ratio: 6 to 8 parent/child units per instructor.

Suggestion: Aquatic staff holds program orientation meeting for first-time parents (without children) prior to each new session.

Lesson 1
1. Introduce staff (name and brief qualifications) to parents and call roll.
2. Review emergency action plan and pool and class rules.
3. Highlight program orientation meeting.
4. Water adjustment:
   a. Sit on edge of pool with parent's support.
   b. Use paint brushes, sponges, and washcloths to drizzle water over body.
5. Water entry, warm-up, and exploring pool.
   a. Parent enters water; instructor provides assistance with infant where needed.
   b. Using "dance" position, bounce/swirl slowly.
   c. Sing a "get wet" song (e.g., "Wheels on the Bus").
6. Introduction of new skills:
   a. Front kick (holding positions: hug and face-to-face: chin support); natural kick; remind parents to say "kick, kick."
   b. Blowing bubbles (dance position)—parent hums and blows against child's hand or cheek.
   c. Prone glide (hug).
   d. Back float (back to chest).
   e. Safety skill: rolling over—back to front.
7. Water exit: ramp or ladder. Instructor assists if necessary.
8. Tapering off.

End each lesson with a fun activity—game or song. Review skills taught and preview what will be introduced during the next lesson.

Lesson 2
1. Water adjustment—Repeat Lesson 1.
2. Water entry and warm-up:
   a. Repeat Lesson 1.
   b. Use tub toys to play with, blow at, and chase.

3. Review:
   a. Front kick.
   b. Blowing bubbles.
   c. Prone glide.
   d. Back float.
4. Introduction of new skills:
   a. Front kick (parent moves child's legs in up-and-down movement).
   b. Underwater exploration: use paint brushes, sponges, wash cloths, etc., and let water flow from back of head toward face.
   c. Safety skills: parent safety—reaching assist.
5. Tapering off:
   a. Game or activity: _____
   b. Review skills introduced in this lesson.
   c. Preview of next lesson.

Toddler Level

Time: Maximum 30 minutes in the water.

Ratio: 6 to 8 parent/child units per instructor.

Suggestion: Aquatic staff holds program orientation meeting for first-time parents (with or without children) prior to each new session.

Lesson 1
1.–4. Same as Infant level.
5. Introduction of new skills:
    a. Front kick (face-to-face: armpit or shoulder support depending on size and readiness)—natural movement.
    b   Blowing bubbles (dance or face-to-face: armpit support).
    c. Prone glide (face-to-face: armpit or shoulder support).
    d. Back float (back to chest or cheek-to-cheek positions).
    e. Safety skill: rolling over—back to front.
6. Water exit: ramp, steps, or ladder.
7. Tapering off:
    a. Game or activity: _____
    b   Review skills introduced in this lesson.
    c. Preview of next lesson.

Lesson 2
1. Water adjustment—Repeat Lesson 1.
2. Water entry and warm-up:
    a. Repeat Lesson 1.
    b   Use of tub toys to play with, blow at, and chase while kicking naturally.
3. Review and practice skills learned in Lesson 1.
4. Introduction of new skills:
    a. Front kick: (hug) parent manipulates child's leg in up-and-down movement.
    b   Underwater exploration: begin experiencing water on face (use paint brushes, sponges, washcloths, sprinkling can).
5. Water exit: climbing out.
6. Tapering off:
    a. Game or activity: _____
    b   Review skills introduced in this lesson.
    c. Preview of next lesson.

Preschool Level

Time: Maximum 45 minutes in the water.

Ratio: 5 to 8 children per instructor.

Suggestion: Aquatic staff holds parent orientation meeting for first-time parents (with children) prior to each new session.

Lesson 1
1. and 2. Same as Infant level.
3. Water adjustment:
    a. Sit on edge of pool and kick; if possible, roll over on front and kick.
    b. Use paint brushes, etc., to drizzle water over body, play "Simon Says."
4. Water entry and warm-up:
    Use one or more—ramp, steps, or ladder unassisted.
5. Introduction of new skills:
    a. Front kick (holding onto side of pool).
    b. Blowing bubbles (holding onto side of pool).
    c. Prone glide: passing—to wall, head up or down.
    d. Rolling over: back to front.
6. Water exit: ladder, ramp, or steps.
7. Tapering off:
    a. Game or activity: _____
    b. Review skills introduced in this lesson.
    c. Preview of next lesson.

Lesson 2
1. and 2. Same as Lesson 1.
3. Review skills introduced in Lesson 1.
4. Introduction of new skills:
    a. Bobbing (holding onto side).
    b. Prone glide—drafting.
    c. Back float (cheek-to-cheek: neck and back support).
    d. Beginning stroke: arm movement (side to side).
    e. Safety skill: rolling over, back to front.
5. Water exit: climbing out.
6. Tapering off:
    a. Game or activity: _____
    b. Review skills introduced in this lesson.
    c. Preview of next lesson.

APPENDIX G

SAMPLE POST-CLASS LETTER TO PARENTS

(Preschool Level)

Note: Sample can be modified and sent on appropriate facility's letterhead.

Dear Mr./Mrs. _____:

I have enjoyed having your child, _____,
participate in the American Red Cross Infant and Preschool Aquatic Program. I hope the lessons were beneficial and enjoyable.

Your child's progress has been recorded below. The skills that your child has successfully completed have been checked. The unchecked skills require additional work. I encourage you to join your child at the many open swim sessions offered at the pool to see his or her progress, and to help your child master any unchecked skills.

_____ Getting face wet
_____ Holding breath underwater: _____ seconds
_____ Rhythmic bobbing: ___ times
_____ Front float: ___ seconds
_____ Front glide: ___ feet
_____ Back glide: ___ feet
_____ Jumping in chest-deep water
_____ Jumping in deep water

Instructor's recommendation:

_____ Your child is ready for Beginner Swimmer lessons. It is important to sign up as soon as possible so that your child can continue to improve his or her skills. In the meantime, the above skills should be practiced. If too much time lapses without practice, your child may need to relearn these skills.

_____ Your child needs additional work at the Preschool level.

Date _____   _____
                                              Instructor

APPENDIX H

PARENTS' EVALUATION

About the Course

1. Which American Red Cross course did you just finish? (Ask your instructor for the correct name.) _____

2. Who taught the course? (List all instructors' names.)

    _____

    _____

3. To what extent do you agree or disagree with the following statements?

Instructor	Strongly Agree	Agree	Not Sure	Dis- Agree	Strongly Disagree
a. The instructor was well prepared.	1	2	3	4	5
b. The instructor knew how to explain things.	1	2	3	4	5
c. The instructor gave my child individual attention.	1	2	3	4	5
d. The instructor answered questions clearly.	1	2	3	4	5

Course					
e. I learned how to help my child in the water.	1	2	3	4	5
f. I learned how to help my child with swimming readiness skills.	1	2	3	4	5
g. I learned how to keep my child safe around water.	1	2	3	4	5
h. I would recommend this American Red Cross course to a friend.	1	2	3	4	5
i. In general, the course met my expectations.	1	2	3	4	5

Time and Equipment

4. Was there enough time to practice?   ___ Yes ___ No
5. Was there enough space?   ___ Yes ___ No
6. Was there enough equipment for everyone?   ___ Yes ___ No
7. Was all the equipment in good condition?   ___ Yes ___ No
8. Were the changing facilities adequate?   ___ Yes ___ No

Some Information About You and Your Child

9. How old is your child? _____ years, _____ months
10. Is your child male or female? _____ male _____ female
11. Do you or any of your close friends or relatives own a pool? ___ yes ___ no
12. Why did you enroll your child in this course?

_____
_____

Comments and Suggestions

13. If you have suggestions or comments, please describe them below.

_____
_____
_____
_____
_____

Thank you for answering these questions. We hope you enjoyed the course.

Chapter Name _____

Date _____

APPENDIX I

INSTRUCTOR CLASS EVALUATION

This appendix contains two copies of the evaluation. Use the first copy the **FIRST** time you teach the course, and the second copy the **FOURTH** time you teach it.

INSTRUCTOR CLASS EVALUATION

The American Red Cross needs your help to continue to improve the Infant and Preschool Aquatic Program (IPAP). Please complete a copy of this evaluation the **FIRST** time you teach the course, and complete another copy the **FOURTH** time you teach it.

Background

1. What is today's date? _____
2. Which level did you teach?
    ❑ Infant (6–18 months)
    ❑ Toddler (18–36 months)
    ❑ Preschool (3 through 5 years)
    ❑ Modification or combination of above
        Please explain _____
3. Number of participants: Adults _____ Children _____
4. Is this your first or fourth time teaching an Infant and Preschool Aquatic Program course?
    ❑ First   ❑ Fourth
5. Which of the following best describes your role in teaching your most recent IPAP course?
    ❑ I taught as a volunteer.
    ❑ I taught as part of my job for the American Red Cross.
    ❑ I taught as part of my job for another organization.
    ❑ I was paid a fee by the Red Cross (per diem instructor).
    ❑ I was paid a fee by another organization (per diem).
6. Length of each lesson: _____ minutes.
7. Number of lessons in the course: _____.
8. Which of the following best describes where you taught the course?
    ❑ Public community pool
    ❑ Private pool (school, association, or neighborhood)
    ❑ Pool at a private residence
    ❑ Other (specify) _____
9. Was the facility used to teach this class: ❑ Indoors   ❑ Outdoors
10. How long have you been a certified American Red Cross water safety instructor (WSI)?
    _____ years.
11. Did you see the IPAP *Training for Instructors* video as part of your WSI class or WSI retraining?   ❑ Yes   ❑ No
12. Have you reviewed that video since your training?   ❑ Yes   ❑ No
    If yes, was it: ❑ Individually   ❑ With other staff members
13. Did you use any of the following:
    Parent's Video ❑ Yes   ❑ No
    Parent's Guide ❑ Yes   ❑ No

Course

14. Do you have any questions about the course that are not answered in the Instructor's Manual? If so, what are they? _____
_____
_____
_____
_____
_____

15. Do you have any suggestions for improving the Instructor's Manual? If so, please list them.
_____
_____
_____
_____
_____
_____

16. Do you have any suggestions for improving the IPAP instructor training videos, the Parent's Video, or the Parent's Guide? If so, please elaborate.
_____
_____
_____
_____
_____
_____

Optional: If you are willing to discuss your comments with us, please give us your name and daytime phone number. We would like to be able to call you if we have any questions.

Name: _____ Phone ( ) _____
Chapter name: _____ City or town: _____

Thank you for taking the time to answer these questions. If you have additional comments about the course, please include them on a separate sheet and attach it to this evaluation.

Please return completed evaluations to—
   American Red Cross
   Health and Safety Division, IPAP
   17th and D Streets, N.W.
   Washington, DC 20006

INSTRUCTOR CLASS EVALUATION

The American Red Cross needs your help to continue to improve the Infant and Preschool Aquatic Program (IPAP). Please complete a copy of this evaluation the **FIRST** time you teach the course, and complete another copy the **FOURTH** time you teach it.

Background

1. What is today's date? _____
2. Which level did you teach?
   ☐ Infant (6–18 months)
   ☐ Toddler (18–36 months)
   ☐ Preschool (3 through 5 years)
   ☐ Modification or combination of above
      Please explain _____
3. Number of participants: Adults _____ Children _____
4. Is this your first or fourth time teaching an Infant and Preschool Aquatic Program course?
   ☐ First   ☐ Fourth
5. Which of the following best describes your role in teaching your most recent IPAP course?
   ☐ I taught as a volunteer.
   ☐ I taught as part of my job for the American Red Cross.
   ☐ I taught as part of my job for another organization.
   ☐ I was paid a fee by the Red Cross (per diem instructor).
   ☐ I was paid a fee by another organization (per diem).
6. Length of each lesson: _____ minutes.
7. Number of lessons in the course: _____.
8. Which of the following best describes where you taught the course?
   ☐ Public community pool
   ☐ Private pool (school, association, or neighborhood)
   ☐ Pool at a private residence
   ☐ Other (specify) _____
9. Was the facility used to teach this class: ☐ Indoors   ☐ Outdoors
10. How long have you been a certified American Red Cross water safety instructor (WSI)?
    _____ years.
11. Did you see the IPAP *Training for Instructors* video as part of your WSI class or WSI retraining?   ☐ Yes   ☐ No
12. Have you reviewed that video since your training?   ☐ Yes   ☐ No
    If yes, was it: ☐ Individually   ☐ With other staff members
13. Did you use any of the following:
    Parent's Video   ☐ Yes   ☐ No
    Parent's Guide   ☐ Yes   ☐ No

Course

14. Do you have any questions about the course that are not answered in the Instructor's Manual? If so, what are they? _____
   _____
   _____
   _____
   _____
   _____

15. Do you have any suggestions for improving the Instructor's Manual? If so, please list them.
   _____
   _____
   _____
   _____
   _____
   _____

16. Do you have any suggestions for improving the IPAP instructor training videos, the Parent's Video, or the Parent's Guide? If so, please elaborate.
   _____
   _____
   _____
   _____
   _____
   _____

Optional: If you are willing to discuss your comments with us, please give us your name and daytime phone number. We would like to be able to call you if we have any questions.

Name: _____ Phone ( )_____
Chapter name: _____ City or town: _____

Thank you for taking the time to answer these questions. If you have additional comments about the course, please include them on a separate sheet and attach it to this evaluation.

Please return completed evaluations to—
   American Red Cross
   Health and Safety Division, IPAP
   17th and D Streets, N.W.
   Washington, DC 20006

Notes

Notes

Notes

Notes